# FINDING YOUR
# IRISH
# ANCESTORS
## UNIQUE ASPECTS
## OF IRISH GENEALOGY

*by*
*Brian Mitchell*

Donegal

Londonderry

Antrim

**ULSTER**

Tyrone

Down

Fermanagh

Armagh

Monaghan

Sligo

Leitrim

Cavan

Louth

Mayo

Roscommon

Longford

Meath

**CONNAUGHT**

Westmeath

Galway

**LEINSTER**

Offaly (Kings)

Dublin

Kildare

Leix
(Queens)

Wicklow

Clare

Carlow

Tipperary

Kilkenny

Limerick

Wexford

**MUNSTER**

Waterford

Kerry

Cork

**CLEARFIELD**

Printed for
Clearfield Company by
Genealogical Publishing Co.
Baltimore, Maryland
2001

Reprinted for
Clearfield Company by
Genealogical Publishing Co.
Baltimore, Maryland
2002, 2003, 2007

ISBN-13: 978-0-8063-5100-1
ISBN-10: 0-8063-5100-4

Made in the United States of America

# CONTENTS

# LIST OF ILLUSTRATIONS

# Introduction

In August 2000 I had the very enjoyable experience of being a guest speaker at the British Isles Family History Society - USA conference on board the legendary Queen Mary, one of the largest passenger liners ever built. Billed as *Down To The Docks: The New World Beckons*, this millennial conference at Long Beach, California, attracted nearly 200 delegates seeking insight and inspiration into researching their English, Irish, Scottish and Welsh ancestors.

The organizers asked me to prepare and present eight talks, of my choosing, on any aspects of Irish genealogy. As there are many excellent "How To" books on tracing Irish ancestry, I felt that I should attempt to give a more personal insight into those genealogical issues that I considered important. Indeed this conference, after I talked to and listened to the stories of dedication and ingenuity demonstrated by delegates in researching their own family histories, confirmed for me that personal qualities such as dedication, patience, perseverance and enthusiasm are just as important, if not more so, than expertise, knowledge and skill in unravelling family history.

I, therefore, decided to base my talks, and as a consequence this book, around research into one Irish family; namely, the Parkhill family from the townland of Gortgare in County Londonderry (also known as Derry). It didn't really matter which family I chose. The issues in tracing your ancestors in Ireland, whether they are from Cork or Derry, or from Dublin or Galway, are essentially the same. It was simply natural for me to pick a family history from County Derry -- the oakleaf county -- as it is my home county. In addition, my working life, as manager of the Derry Genealogy Centre, has been directed towards helping people trace their roots in this county.

In the first chapter -- Tracing Your Irish Ancestors: An Overview -- I have attempted, by tracing the family history of the Parkhill family, to raise those issues which I consider are central to a fulfilling genealogical search.

These issues are then examined in greater detail in the remainder of the book. Surnames and place names in Ireland should be seen for what they are, a treasure trove of historical information stretching back over one thousand years. On many occasions I have felt that people have missed the clues, and more importantly the enjoyment, provided by studying surnames and place names in their determination to begin searching actual record sources. In this results-driven world, we seem to have lost the art of learning from and enjoying the journey itself.

I, for example, find great inspiration in the huge entrance hall and reception area of Derry City Council's new headquarters as set in the ceiling are 80 colourful crests representing many of North West Ireland's most famous families. The history of Derry over the past millennium can be visualized in these coats of arms depicting the major Gaelic clans of the area such as Doherty, McLaughlin and O'Donnell; the original guilds of the City of London such as the Fishmongers', Goldsmiths' and Grocers' Companies; business names such as Tillie, Coppin, McCorkell and

Cooke; political and historical names of Walker, Cairns, Lundy, Murray and Knox; and literary and musical names of Heaney, Coulter and Friel.

There is a great fascination in identifying ancestors in passenger lists. Owing to limited information recorded in many passenger lists, finding your ancestor in them will be of more sentimental than genealogical value. On the other hand, however, any attempts to examine the trends in Irish emigration over the past three centuries will be rewarded with some insight into why your ancestors emigrated and why they settled where they did.

I cannot emphasize enough the importance of examining record sources in North America before embarking on research in Irish record sources. The more precise your knowledge of where your ancestor lived in Ireland, ideally a parish or townland address, the better your chances of a worthwhile family search. Most record sources in Ireland were organized, and consequently are now accessed, by parish. The knowledge of an even more localised townland address effectively means you could visit the ancestral home. In short, all potential record sources in the USA and Canada should be examined for clues as to a place of origin in Ireland of your immigrant ancestor.

The most significant record source in Ireland, in terms of making and confirming family links back in time, are church registers of baptisms and marriages. Again, knowledge of where your ancestor lived is crucial for effective research of church registers. To conduct a realistic search of church registers in Ireland, in the absence of any indexes, you need to know a civil parish address of your ancestor. Thus any clues to the place of origin of your ancestor in Ireland, whether it be gleaned from family knowledge or from an examination of record sources in your home country, should be carefully recorded.

Don't despair, however, if you feel you have exhausted all avenues in your attempts to find out where your ancestor came from in Ireland. The databases being built up by the network of genealogy centres, usually established on a county basis, may provide some answers for those with insufficient place information to select record sources to search.

I firmly believe that the family historian can gain much from a local historian with an interest in exploring the community which lived in a particular place. Not only might a local historian have identified some information about your particular ancestor, but he or she can provide insight into what conditions -- whether they be political, economic, social or cultural -- were like in the area in which your ancestors resided.

Finally, always remember, in the words of an old Gaelic proverb: *No door ever closed, but another opened.* There are always opportunities for exploring new avenues in researching your Irish roots.

## Tracing Your Irish Ancestors
## An Overview

"If you understand a man the first time you meet him, there isn't much in him to understand. And you won't understand Robert McCook at the start, for he is an Irishman, and a deep one at that. A big lump of a man - 6 feet 2 inches in his socks - broad, thick-chested, going bald on top. You'd pick him out as a farmer if you met him on board ship or in a cafe in Paris. He looks the part." This is how the *Dairy Bulletin* of June 1910 described Robert McCook, then the owner of a big herd of Jersey milking cows in Brisbane, Australia, but formerly a farmer's son from Garvagh, County Londonderry. With this information I began my research, with the assistance of my father-in-law, into the McCook families of Ireland, Australia and New Zealand, and what a story it turned out to be.

Two Sunday afternoon chats around the fireside with 87-year-old Robert Graham, who owned the McCook farm in Garvagh, enabled us to virtually tie up the McCook family tree in Ireland for descendants of McCooks living in New Zealand and Australia. Robert, leaning slightly forward on his walking stick, his eyes bright with recollection, recalled for a total of six hours the McCook family history.

This one example sums up for me the very essence of genealogy, namely that the chase is as rewarding, if not more so, than the end results. Qualities such as persistence, dedication and enthusiasm come to the fore in any genealogical quest. The McCook story also confirms my belief that worthwhile genealogical research begins with identifying any information, including anecdotes, that relatives, family friends or neighbours may hold. In addition to recording oral tradition, a search should be made through family papers to unearth old photographs, newspaper clippings with perhaps an obituary, letters, or even a family bible with its own family tree within.

I would also recommend, prior to any systematic search of record sources, the recording of any information you have gathered in pedigree or family charts. These charts, which you can either purchase or design yourself, will not only summarise the information you hold but will also highlight where further research is needed. By identifying at a glance, gaps in your knowledge, an up-to-date pedigree chart acts as a framework for future research.

By the time you've contacted your relatives, located any old family documents and recorded all this information on pedigree charts, you should have built up an outline family tree detailing names, locations and dates. Only now should you consider identifying and searching record sources.

For those of Irish descent in Canada and the USA the tracing of your Irish roots doesn't begin in Ireland (see chapter on *Using Record Sources in the US and Canada to identify your Irish Ancestors*). It begins in your home country. It is only by building up a picture of your ancestors in their adopted country will you find the necessary clues to make a worthwhile search in Ireland. I would summarise the search into your Irish family history origins as follows:

# The Family History Process

| | |
|---|---|
| ORAL TRADITION | Quiz relatives - not only is this enjoyable, it saves time spent on wasteful searches for information already known. |
| FAMILY PAPERS | Photographs<br>Newspaper Cuttings<br>Family Bible |
| RECORD INFORMATION | Names    )    in family<br>Dates     )    history file<br>Places    )    or Personal Computer |
| PEDIGREE CHART | Only allows for the recording of direct line ancestors. Solution - construct your own family tree. |
| FRAMEWORK | By Condensing your knowledge on one piece of paper it highlights areas requiring further research. |
| SEARCH KNOWN INDEXES | International Genealogical Index (IGI) now accessible on the internet at www.familysearch.org<br>Published Indexes<br>Indexes in Irish Record Offices<br>Databases (for a fee) of Ireland's Genealogy Centres. |
| BEGIN RECORD SEARCH | Civil birth, marriage & death registers<br>Church baptismal, marriage & burial records<br>Graveyards<br>1901 and 1911 census<br>Mid-19th century Griffith's Valuation<br>Early-19th century Tithe Books<br>18th-century (and earlier) Census substitutes, such as 1796 Flax Lists, 1766 Religious Census, 1740 Protestant Householders Lists and 1663 Hearth Money Rolls.<br>Estate Records - Leases, Rentals and Surveys<br>*Information gathered on names, dates, places and family connections act as clues to further sources to search.* |
| UPDATE | Family History File and Pedigree charts updated as new information found. |

I intend to use the Parkhill family of Gortgare, County Londonderry (also known as Derry) as an example of tracing Irish ancestry.

Irish Family History Research begins with your surname (see chapter on *The Importance of Surnames in Family History*). The only tangible link that many people of Irish descent in Canada and the US retain with Ireland is their family name. Your surname can provide clues and insights into the origins of ones family history. I would always recommend an examination of surname reference books to find out as much as you can about the origins of surnames in your family tree. Irish surnames, whether of Gaelic-Irish or of Scottish and English origin, frequently provide clues to a place of origin, as many names have a territorial basis.

The surname Parkhill is ultimately derived from the lands of Parkhill in Ayrshire, Scotland. The lands along the Firth of Clyde in the old county of Ayrshire, stretching from Largs in the north through Ardrossan, Irvine, Kilmarnock, Troon, Ayr, Turnberry, Girvan and Ballantrae in the south, are the homeland of many who settled in County Londonderry during the17th century Plantation of Ulster.

Surnames, ie an inherited family name, are the building blocks of genealogy - without them it would be impossible to trace back through the generations. Clearly, successful genealogical research rests on the correct interpretation of surnames from historical records. Poor handwriting and the poor condition of many church registers, for example, can cause problems of interpretation.

The key to unlocking your family history origins is a knowledge of place (see chapter on *The Importance of Place in Family History*). For practical genealogical purposes Ireland is subdivided into counties which in turn are subdivided into parishes which in turn are subdivided into townlands. As a general rule the knowledge of the county of origin of your ancestor is insufficient evidence for locating them.

The TOWNLAND INDEX confirms that the townland of Gortgare is located in the civil parish of Faughanvale, County Londonderry (see map of civil parishes on page 26). County Londonderry is subdivided into 46 civil parishes. As most records of genealogical value were compiled by civil parish it means that effective genealogical research in Ireland requires knowledge of the civil parish in which your ancestor lived. As the parish report for Faughanvale Parish shows (see parish report on page 32) the selection of appropriate records to search becomes self-evident.

It is a strong driving force among most people tracing their family history to identify an ancestral home. In Ireland this in effect means identifying the townland your ancestor lived in. The townland is the smallest and most ancient of Irish land divisions, and its identification is essential to researchers who wish to pinpoint the precise origin of their ancestors. There are 66 townlands in the parish of Faughanvale (see map of townlands on page 29 ). The Parkhill family, in our example, lived in the townland of Gortgare (which means "the short field"). This townland, which is 279 acres in size, can be located on Sheet 15 of the 6 inch Ordnance Survey Map for County Londonderry.

The story of emigration from Ireland to North America is one of the most fascinating and significant aspects of Irish history of the past three centuries (see chapter on *Emigration and Irish Passenger Lists*). In 1857 a Robert Parkhill, age 18, emigrated from the port of Derry on the ship Argentinus to Quebec, Canada. According to the passenger lists of the local shipping company J & J Cooke (published in *Irish Passenger Lists 1847-1871* by the Genealogical Publishing Company) Robert Parkhill's address was Ballykelly. The addresses recorded in the order books of J & J Cooke were generally those of the nearest village or town to where the emigrant actually lived. The townland of Gortgare is located some 4 miles to the west of the small town of Ballykelly.

In the middle years of the 19th century the cheapest way to cross the Atlantic was on a J & J Cooke sailing ship out of Derry. Owing to her westerly situation it was said that a Derry sailing ship bound for North America "is no sooner out of the river, but she is immediately in the open sea and has but one course".

We are now ready to begin searching record sources. Genealogy now becomes the art of linking records to together. Civil registration in Ireland of births, deaths and Roman Catholic marriages began in January 1864 while Protestant marriages were subject to registration from April 1845. If your ancestor was born or married after these dates I would always recommend the search of civil birth and marriage registers as your first step. The information in civil death registers is from a genealogical point of view quite disappointing. A death certificate provides the deceased's name, age, occupation, cause of death and place of death.

Birth certificates provide the name, date of birth and place of birth of the child, together with the father's name, occupation and residence and the mother's name and maiden name. A marriage certificate provides the names, ages, marital status, occupations and residences of the bride and groom, together with the names and occupations of their fathers. The date and place of marriage and the names of two witnesses are also included. These civil certificates clearly supply enough information to build and confirm family linkages. A marriage certificate, for example, provides information on four direct ancestors and two branches of the family tree. Furthermore, all-Ireland indexes provide convenient access to civil registers.

In this case the marriage certificate of Samuel Parkhill, of full age (ie over 21 years), a farmer of Gortgarr confirms that he married Jane Morrow, of full age, of Termacoy in Faughanvale Presbyterian Church on 20 September 1849. The certificate records that Samuel's father was Robert Parkhill and Jane's, James Morrow. The witnesses were Robert Morrow and Robert Parkhill.

Prior to the commencement of civil registration you will have to rely on church registers (see chapter on *How to make the best use of Church Registers*) to confirm birth and marriage details. Dates of commencement and quality of information in church baptismal, marriage and burial registers vary from parish to parish and from denomination to denomination. Access to church registers is gained through knowledge of the parish address and religious denomination of your ancestor. If all you know is that your ancestor came from County Londonderry this effectively means that your ancestor could have worshipped in any one of 53 Church of Ireland parishes, 68 Presbyterian congregations or 28 Roman Catholic parishes that were in existence in the county prior to 1900.

In our example an examination of the registers of Faughanvale Presbyterian Church would seem to be a natural starting point. No marriage registers for Faughanvale Presbyterian church predate civil registration (ie 1845). Baptism registers for this congregation, however, do date back to 1819. These registers record that a Samuel Parkhill was born on 28 October 1853 to parents Samuel and Jane Parkhill of Gortgar. It also records the births of siblings Margaret (on 17 May 1850), William James (3 December 1851), Jane (6 February 1856) and Robert (1 September 1858).

Care and patience are great virtues when it comes to examining church registers. Some church registers, especially of a later date, may be tabulated and the information written in the appropriate columns, neatly and legibly. But often the information is simply written, and not too clearly at that, in sentence form. The implications for the impatient will be to overlook the very entry you are looking for.

With civil registration of births and deaths commencing in 1864, and with the patchy survival of church records prior to 1820, gravestone inscriptions take on a special significance. Many Church of Ireland burial registers were destroyed by fire in the Public Record Office, Dublin in 1922, while the registers of the Roman Catholic and Presbyterian churches are especially poor regarding burial entries. In many cases a gravestone inscription will be the only record of an ancestor's death. But gravestones offer much more than just the date of death; they frequently mention the townland address of the deceased together with the names, ages, and dates of death of other family members. Many graves are family plots and as a consequence list family members and their relationship to each other. In some instances a family tree comprising three generations can be constructed.

Church of Ireland graveyards should be examined irrespective of an ancestor's religion. Prior to the 1820s, owing to the operation of the Penal Laws, both Catholics and Presbyterians shared the same graveyards. And prior to the Burial Act of 1868, which permitted dissenting (ie Presbyterian) ministers to conduct burial services, the Church of Ireland clergy held jurisdiction over funeral services for all Protestants. This in effect means that the graveyards of both Faughanvale Church of Ireland and Faughanvale Presbyterian churches need to be examined in our search for Parkhills of Gortgare. It is, unfortunately, true that the unkempt state of many graveyards (especially those now isolated from a functioning church) and the weathering of headstones precludes the reading of many inscriptions.

No Parkhill burial plots could be found in the Church of Ireland graveyard. Two headstones were located in the graveyard of Faughanvale Presbyterian Church for Parkhill families of Greysteel and Dungullion. It would seem, however, that in this instance gravestone inscriptions will shed no additional light on the Parkhills of Gortgare.

Although census enumerations were carried out every decade from 1821, the earliest surviving complete return for all Ireland is that of 1901. This census provides for each member of the household their name, age, religion, education, occupation, marital status and county or city of birth. The 1911 census provides additional information on the marriage; namely the number of years married, the number of children born and the number still living.

In 1901 Jane Parkhill, a widow, age 65 and children Margaret, William James, Samuel and Jane were living in Gortgare (Jane's husband Samuel Parkhill, therefore, was dead by 1901). Based on the age recorded in the 1901 census it would seem that Jane Morrow was born c. 1836. By the time of the 1911 census siblings (all unmarried) Samuel, William James, Jane and Mary were residing in one household in Gortgare. It would seem that their mother, Jane, died sometime between 1901 and 1911.

Ages recorded in census records should only be used as a guide. For example in the Parkhill family of Gortgare, according to the census, Samuel Parkhill, aged 23 years (from age 32 to 55) in the ten year period, 1901 to 1911, while William James aged 19 years (from 34 to 53) and Jane 20 years (from 30 to 50).

Owing to the destruction of most early-19th century and mid-19th century census returns in Ireland, the Tithe Applotment books and Griffith's Valuation are records of extreme importance to family researchers. They are, in effect, census substitutes for pre-Famine and post-Famine Ireland respectively.

The Tithe Applotment Books, compiled between 1823 and 1837, list all landholders who paid tithe (tax) to the Established Church (ie Church of Ireland). The Griffith's Valuation was a survey carried out between 1848 and 1864 that detailed every head of household and occupier of land in Ireland. Once you know the townland address of your ancestor it is relatively easy to examine the 1901 census, Griffith's Valuation and Tithe Books to identify changes in households through the 19th century. The major limitation of the Tithe and Griffith's valuations is the fact that they record heads of household only. As no information is provided on family members within each household or relationships between householders it is not possible to confirm the nature of linkages between named people in these sources.

The Griffith's Valuation for Faughanvale Parish was published in 1858. This source records households headed by Robert Parkhill senior, Robert Parkhill junior and Samuel Parkhill living and farming in the townland of Gortgare in 1858. Our previous research would suggest (but the Griffith's Valuation can't confirm it) that Robert Parkhill senior and son, Samuel were jointly farming 37 acres in Gortgare in the middle years of the 19th century.

The Tithe Book for Faughanvale Parish, published in 1835, records Parkhill households headed by Adam, Mary, Robert and Robert farming in Gortgare in this time period. Again the Tithe Book provides insufficient information to confirm the nature of the link between these 4 households.

If you are fortunate that early-19th century census returns survive for the townland your ancestor lived in then they should also be searched. County Londonderry is fortunate in this regard as a copy of the 1831 census exists. However, it only records heads of households. In 1831 Parkhill families headed by Adam, Mary, Robert and William Junior resided in Gortgare. According to the census all these families were Presbyterian.

As maps were compiled to accompany the Griffith's Valuation this means that the locations of all properties in the mid-19th century - houses and farms - can be identified once you have found your ancestor in the actual Griffith's Valuation. In other words with these maps you can identify with accuracy the location of the ancestral home (even if it is now long gone) or farm. Householders with no land (such as agricultural labourers or town dwellers) are also identified on the Griffith's Valuation maps.

Every lot number in the Griffith's Valuation (recorded under the heading "No. and Letters of Reference to Map") was marked on a copy of the Ordnance Survey map (at a scale of 6" to 1 mile) at the Valuation Office, Dublin. Copies of the Griffith's Valuation maps for the 26 counties of the Republic of Ireland can be found in the Valuation Office, Irish Life Centre, Abbey Street Lower, Dublin while those for the 6 counties of Northern Ireland are held in the Public Record Office of Northern Ireland, 66 Balmoral Avenue, Belfast.

The ancestral home of the Parkhills in Middle Gortgare can be easily located on the Griffith's Valuation map which in turn means it can be identified and visited. In this farmhouse, overlooking Lough Foyle and Inishowen, Jane Parkhill and family were living in 1901. In the 1901 census the Parkhill farmhouse, consisting of 5 rooms with five windows to the front, with walls of stone or brick and roof of slate, iron or tiles, was described as a second class house. The farm had seven outhouses consisting of a stable, cow house, calf house, piggery, boiling house, barn and shed.

By examining a range of maps (at a scale of 6 inches to one mile) over time for Gortgare such as the 1st Valuation map of 1834, the Griffith's Valuation map of 1858 and the 1907 edition of the Ordnance Survey map changes in settlement patterns and farm units can be followed. For example Robert Barber's farm of 68 acres in 1858 consisted of 5 farms at the time of the 1st Valuation map of 1834. In 1858 the settlement of Upper Gortgare housed 6 families, by 1907 there was no physical trace of this small hamlet.

As no church baptismal, marriage or burial registers predate 1802 in the civil parish of Faughanvale it is highly unlikely that you will be able to link with any degree of certainty Parkhill connections back through the 18th century. There are still a number of sources you can search for references to the Parkhill name but it will be difficult to prove the nature of the relationship between any Parkhills that are identified.

Prior to the 1900s the majority of the Irish population lived on large estates. Many landlords of these estates kept records in which details of tenants' leases, rent payments and other such matters were recorded. The townland of Gortgare, for example, was granted in the 17th century to the Fishmongers Company of London. Records of this estate are held in the Public Record Office, Belfast ( reference D1118, T2607/1-2 and MIC9B/11, 17, 18 and 19). These estate records include rentals, court minutes, land agreements, accounts and wage books with the earliest record dating to 1613. It is possible that Parkhill details might be recorded among this vast collection of records. It requires patience and care to search sources such as these. It must also be pointed out that there is no formula which will predict a successful search of such sources.

There are also a number of census records and census substitutes which could be searched. Sources which list heads of household in Faughanvale Parish include the private census of 1803, the Flax Growers' Lists of 1796, the Protestant Householders Lists of 1740 and the Hearth Money Rolls of 1663. These sources should be searched for all references to Parkhill. Again there will be insufficient information to confirm the nature of the link between say Parkhills recorded in the 1796 Flax Lists and those recorded in the 1740 Protestant Householders Lists. For example the Protestant Householders Lists of 1740 record two Parkhill heads of household in Faughanvale Parish in 1740, namely Samuel Parkhill and Robert Parkhill in the townland of Greysteel. This townland adjoins that of Gortgare. It is almost certain that these Parkhills are directly related to the Parkhills of Gortgare (but we can't prove it).

At the time of the Hearth Money Rolls of 1663 no Parkhills were recorded in the parish of Faughanvale. It is quite feasible (but again we can't prove it) that the Parkhills settled in Faughanvale Parish towards the end of the 17th century. History certainly confirms that substantial numbers of Scottish families entered the province of Ulster, through the port of Derry, and settled in the Foyle Valley, especially in the 1690s, following the cessation of the Williamite wars. It is said, that in 1691 alone, 10,000 left Scotland to settle in Ulster.

There is a growing interest in Ireland in local history. When researching your Irish ancestors it is always a good idea to identify if any books have been researched and written about the locality in which your ancestor resided (see chapter on *Local History and the Family Historian*). For example two books have been produced recently on various aspects of the history of Faughanvale Parish. In 1994 Dr J R White produced a history of Faughanvale Presbyterian Church in his book *The Meeting House at Tullanee*. This book records (on page 25) that Samuel Parkhill of Gortgar Top subscribed £1 0s 0d to Faughanvale Presbyterian Church in the period 1854-59.

*Historic Eglinton a thriving ornament* (by Brian Mitchell) was also published in 1994. As well as recording the history of the village of Eglinton, which is located in the parish of Faughanvale, this book contains muster rolls dating from 1643 and 1800 for the Faughanvale area.

Finally, of real significance to those people tracing their ancestors in Ireland has been the establishment of a network of genealogy centres, usually on a county basis, with unrivalled local databases and the capability to respond to family history queries within their catchment areas (see chapter on *Genealogy Centres in Ireland: How to make the best use of them*).

If you lack the time, sufficient information and/or access to record sources to pursue your family history it makes very good sense to commission a genealogy centre to search their database and compile a report into your family history.

To sum up, once you know the parish and/or townland your ancestor originated from it gives you access to a whole range of genealogical sources. Confirmation, furthermore, of a townland address will enable you to visit the ancestral homeland, talk to local people and perhaps even identify a family homestead.

# The Importance of Surnames in Family History

Irish Family History research begins with your surname. The only tangible link that many people of Irish descent in Canada and the US retain with Ireland is their family name. Your forbears may have left Ireland more than 200 years ago, but with the passage of time your exact ancestry may have become obscured. In your name, however, lies the one sure link with your past - a direct line through many generations to a faraway time and distant place. Your Irish name connects you with a rich and fascinating culture. Each surname has its own story, its own history and geography which can be easily grasped. People generally proclaim their Irish ancestry with pride.

In the city of Londonderry (also known as Derry), where I was born, the top three surnames, today, in descending order are Doherty, McLaughlin and Gallagher. These three surnames all have their origins in the adjoining county of Donegal. The industrial and commercial growth of 19th century Derry drew many people from rural Donegal to settle in the city. Over 1,000 years of recorded history can be seen in surnames such as these. For example the history of the Doherty sept can be traced from their descent from Conall Gulban, son of the 5th century High King of Ireland, Niall of the Nine Hostages to the present-day claimant of the title "The O'Doherty", one Ramon Salvador O'Doherty of San Fernando, Spain. If your name is Doherty you can identify Inishowen in County Donegal as your homeland and that the last chief of the name, Cahir, in ransacking Derry in 1608, paved the way for the Plantation of Ulster.

McLaughlin, the second most popular name in Derry, is derived from the Norse personal name Lachlan.. This County Donegal sept trace their lineage from another of Niall of the Nine Hostages' sons, namely Eoghan. In the 12th century the McLaughlins, from their Inishowen homeland, were the High Kings of Ireland and patrons of the prestigious monastic settlement in Derry. From the mid-13th century the O'Neills of Tyrone ousted the McLaughlins as the leading power in Ulster.

Gallagher, the number three name in present-day Derry, traces its lineage to Eoghan's brother, Conall Gulban. Controlling extensive territories stretching from Raphoe to Ballyshannon, County Donegal, the Gallaghers were the chief marshals in the army of the O'Donnell, Prince of Tirconnell.

On a visit to New Brunswick, Canada in 1991 I was struck by how surnames clearly demonstrated the strength of Irish settlement in this area. The Catholic graveyard in Johnville, an Irish settlement of the 1860s in the Upper St John river valley, has tombstone inscriptions of Doherty, McLaughlin, Gallagher, Gormley, O'Donnell, Murphy, Donovan, Sullivan and O'Brien. In these surnames it is evident that the Irish who settled in New Brunswick came from two main regions: Northwest Ireland, in particular Derry and Donegal, (as evidenced by the first five surnames) and southwest Ireland, especially Cork (as evidenced by the latter 4 surnames).

Ireland's dynamic history can be seen in the richness and variety of its surnames. An examination of the local telephone directory records 1,860 distinct surnames in

Derry city. Each of these surnames bears a distinctive history and taken as a whole they are a record of population movements into the Derry area over the past 400 years. Most of the major Gaelic-Irish sept names and Scottish Clan names can be found in Derry.

The surnames of such great Scottish clans as McDonald, McAllister, McGregor, McKenzie, Sutherland, Cameron, Campbell and Stewart are all recorded in the city. As Lords of the Isles with territory stretching from the Outer Hebrides to Kintyre the McDonalds, for example, became the most powerful clan in Scotland. The Lordship was broken up by the Scottish Crown in 1493. Throughout the 17th century they vied with the Campbells for the position of "Headship of the Gael". The McGregors can trace their descent from Kenneth McAlpine, the 9th century King of Scotland. This clan came to control large territories in Perthshire and Argyllshire but in doing so they came into conflict with the powerful Clan Campbell.

At the height of their power in the 16th century neither the English nor Scottish crowns could control the forays of the so-called riding clans of the Borders of Scotland for cattle and loot. Pacification of these clans began in 1603 with the Union of the Crowns of England and Scotland. Substantial numbers of Scottish families thus entered Ulster through Derry and settled in the Foyle Valley. The end result being that names such as Armstrong (who at the height of their power could muster an army of 3,000 men), Scott, Elliot, Kerr, Nixon and Irvine are common names in the city.

Many surnames of the city, furthermore, are ultimately derived from English place names. Surnames such as Appleby, Ashford, Bamford, Baxendale, Blackburn, Blackwell, Blackwood, Clinton, Furness, Horwill, Kirby, Pemberton, Podmore, Skeffington and Strickland would denote that ultimately the origins of these names derive from very specific places in England.

This wealth and variety of surnames in the city today reflects the fact that from the 17th century Derry was a magnet to Irish, English and Scottish settlers.

In the 20th century Derry has become an even more cosmopolitan place. Surnames such as Battisti, Yanerelli and Firoentini; and of Schenkel, Szilagyi, Spain and Watchman resulted from the arrival of pre-World War Two Italian and Jewish immigrants respectively in Derry. In the post-war period Indian families, mostly from the Punjab, with names such as Chada, Singh, Vig and Vij; and Chinese families, mainly from Hong Kong, with names such as Cheung, Fam, Fan, Ho and Wong, settled in Derry.

In short in any attempt to trace your family history you should always try to find out as much as you can about the origins of the surnames in your family tree. Irish surnames, whether of Gaelic-Irish or of Scottish and English origin, frequently provide clues to a place of origin, as many names have a territorial basis. Most Gaelic-Irish surnames confirm membership of a sept, which is defined as a group of persons, bearing a common surname and with ancestral origins in the same locality. This was previously demonstrated with brief histories of the surnames Doherty,

McLaughlin and Gallagher. Thus surnames reinforce an Irishman's identity with place. Even today Gaelic-Irish surnames are still very dominant and numerous in the very districts where their names originated. This, of course, has implications for the genealogist. One commentator stated: "all to often Celtic Genealogy gets lost in the confusion of too many people with a single surname, with inadequate records to distinguish who is who".

On the other hand, it is generally accepted that members of an Irish sept have a common tribal ancestor. Your place in Gaelic-Irish society was to a large extent dependent on your genealogy. As a consequence the oldest recorded genealogies in the Western World are to be found in Ireland. The major Gaelic-Irish family names have reliable genealogies dating from the 6th century when historical fact begins to take over from origin-legend. For example the present Lord O'Neill (Raymond Arthur Clanaboy O'Neill, 4th Baron O'Neill) of Shane's Castle, County Antrim can trace his lineage back 50 generations to the 5th century Niall of the Nine Hostages.

Between the 4th and 7th centuries AD, Ireland underwent a series of large-scale changes which saw the emergence of new ruling dynasties, as the earlier peoples were pushed into the background, and the penetration of Christianity into the country. From the 7th and 8th centuries Christian monks began to record the ancient, pagan tales of tribal myth, origin-legend and genealogical descent which prior to this had been preserved orally in verse and song. To legitimise the rise to power of new tribal or dynastic groups Gaelic genealogists often forged a link between the usurper and the dynasty they had overthrown. Genealogies were also constructed which connected with Christian tradition and history as revealed in the Bible. Thus the genealogies of the emerging dynastic groups were extended back to Noah and to Adam. Thus the 5th century Niall of the Nine Hostages' lineage was traced back through 87 generations to Adam and Eve.

Ireland was one of the first countries to adopt a system of hereditary surnames which developed from a more ancient system of clan names. From the 11th century families began to adopt their own distinctive family names, generally derived from the first name of an ancestor who lived in or about the 10th century. The surname was formed by prefixing either Mac (son of) or O (grandson or ancestor of) to the ancestor's name.

In attempting to use your ancestor's surname history as a clue to locating their place of origin in Ireland care must be taken. For example, it was quite common for the same surname in Gaelic Ireland to arise independently in different parts of the country. For example the surname Kelly came into being independently in at least seven widely separated places in Ireland, with the most powerful sept being the O'Kellys of Hy Maine who ruled over much of Galway and Roscommon. In Ulster a Kelly sept, claiming descent from Colla, the 4th century King of Ulster, was based in South Derry.

Although Gaelic-Irish surnames are still most dominant in the very districts in which they originated it doesn't necessarily mean that this is where your ancestor (of that name) resided prior to emigration. Although ultimately your ancestor's origins may be from this precise district it is possible that your ancestor had settled elsewhere in Ireland prior to emigration.

Surnames, furthermore, can have more than one ethnic origin. From the 17th century Gaelic surnames were anglicised. Some names were translated into English while others were changed to a similar-sounding English name. This process of anglicisation, together with illiteracy, gave rise to numerous spelling variations of the same name. For example the Derry genealogy centre database has 83 recorded variant spellings of Doherty. You are treading on very thin ice if you assume that because your name is spelt a certain way today then that was the way it was always spelt. Uniformity in spelling surnames is really a phenomenon of the 20th century. The clergy, in entering relevant details on say a baptism register, often had to write down names based on pronunciation as many people could not write down or spell their name. Names of Gaelic origin were, furthermore, disguised by the widespread discarding of the prefixes Mac, Mc and O in the 18th century.

Anglicisation will, in many cases, obscure the true origin of a surname. For example, Smith may be an English surname or an anglicisation of the Gaelic McGowan (meaning son of Smith). My own surname, Mitchell, could have originated independently in England, Lowland Scotland, Highland Scotland or Ireland; only detailed family history research will confirm the actual origin.

A useful step, therefore, in tracing your family history is to be aware of possible variants of your family name. Many surname variants are obvious, for example Docherty, Dogherty and O'Doherty are variants of Doherty. Others are not so obvious: for example in the baptismal registers of Limavady Roman Catholic Parish, County Derry the following entries can be found:

| Child | Father | Mother | Address |
|---|---|---|---|
| Michael | Bernard Kilky | Ellen Logue | Slaughmanus |
| Jane | Bernard Small | Ellen Logue | Slaughtmanus |
| James | Bernard Smalley | Ellen Logue | Slaghtmanus |

Around 1900 (according to Robert Bell's *The book of Ulster Surnames*, Blackstaff Press, Belfast, 1988) the surname Small was being used interchangeably with Kielty, Kilkey and Gilkie.

There will always be instances where potential variant spellings of a surname cannot be predicted; this usually happens when mistakes are made by the official recording the information. For example in the Tithe Book and 1901 census return the surname Governor of Moneydig, County Derry was spelled correctly, but in the Griffith's Valuation the surname was recorded as McGovern.

It is, therefore, always a good idea to consult surname reference books in order to identify potential variants. Such books include:

*Irish Families* by Edward MacLysaght (Irish Academic Press, Dublin, 1985)
*More Irish Families* by Edward MacLysaght (Irish Academic Press, Dublin, 1996)

*The Surnames of Ireland* by Edward MacLysaght (Irish Academic Press, Dublin, 1978)
*The book of Ulster Surnames* by Robert Bell (Blackstaff Press, Belfast, 1988)
*The Surnames of Scotland* by George Black (The New York Public Library, New York, 1986)
*A Dictionary of Surnames* by Patrick Hanks & Flavia Hodges (Oxford University Press, Oxford, 1990)
*A Dictionary of British Surnames* by P H Reaney (Routledge & Kegan Paul, London, 1976)
*The Concise Oxford Dictionary of English Place-names* by Eilert Ekwall (Oxford University Press, Oxford, 1990)

Surnames, ie an inherited family name, are the building blocks of genealogy - without them it would be impossible to trace back through the generations. Clearly, successful genealogical research rests on the correct interpretation of surnames from historical records. Poor handwriting and the poor condition of many church registers can cause problems of interpretation. For example the Thurles Parish Indexing project in County Tipperary found that it was often difficult to distinguish Phelan from Whelan, Bourke from Rourke and Kelly from Kiely in their registers.

The 17th century Plantation of Ulster whuch drew many settlers from both England and Scotland introduced many new surnames to Ireland. Pacification of the riding families of the Borders (who lived by cattle stealing and kidnapping) which began in earnest from 1603 with the Union of the Crowns of England and Scotland; religious conflict in South-West Scotland in the late 1670s which culminated in the severe persecution of Presbyterians, in the so-called "Killing Times", in Ayrshire in the period 1684-1688; and four successive harvest failures, in the 1690s, throughout both the Highlands and the Lowlands, all generated successive waves of Scottish emigrants to Ulster (see map of Scotland showing counties).

English settlers, mostly drawn from the northern counties of Cheshire, Cumberland, Lancashire, Northumberland, Yorkshire and Westmorland tended to favour settlement along the Lagan Valley in the east of the Province (see map of England showing counties).

The London Companies who planted much of County Derry found it hard to hold their ill-prepared and ill-suited English settlers. The Companies, therefore, looked to the durable Scottish farmer to tenant their estates. As a consequence surnames of Scottish origin dominate the Plantation names of the Derry area and owing to the Highland influence many of these names have Gaelic origins. By the end of the 17th century, through waves of migration, a self-sustaining settlement of English and Scottish colonists had established itself in Ulster.

Studies of surname distribution can shed, therefore, much useful light on the nature of English and Scottish settlement in 17th century Ulster. It is descendants of these settlers, the so-called Ulster Scots, who emigrated in large numbers from Ulster ports from 1718 to North America.

# SCOTLAND

## COUNTIES BEFORE 1975

**SCOTLAND**
COUNTIES BEFORE 1975

Orkney Islands

Shetland Islands

Caithness

OUTER
Lewis
Sutherland

HEBRIDES

N. Uist

Ross and Cromarty

Nairn
Moray
Banff
Aberdeen

S. Uist
Skye
Inverness

Kincardine

INNER

Angus

Perth

Mull
Argyll
Clackmannan
Fife
Kinross

HEBRIDES
Jura
Dunbarton
Stirling
West Lothian
East Lothian
Midlothian
Renfrew
Berwick

Islay
Lanark
Peebles

Bute
Selkirk
Arran
Ayr
Roxburgh

Dumfries

Kirkcudbright
Wigtown

IRELAND
ENGLAND

15

ENGLAND AND WALES

COUNTIES BEFORE 1975

ENGLAND AND WALES
COUNTIES BEFORE 1975

SCOTLAND

IRELAND

Northumberland

Cumberland       Durham

Westmorland

Isle
of Man                          Yorkshire

Lancashire

Anglesey
                    Flint
Caernarvon   Denbigh       Cheshire    Derby    Nottingham    Lincoln
            Merioneth
                            Stafford              Rutland
         Montgomery                   Leicester                    Norfolk
                    Shropshire
                                          Warwick   Huntingdon   Cambridge
         Cardigan    Radnor      Worcester      Northampton              Suffolk
Pembroke           Brecknock   Hereford                  Bedford
      Carmarthen                                  Oxford   Buckingham   Hertford   Essex
              Monmouth      Gloucester
      Glamorgan                                              Greater
                                                             London
                                     Wiltshire   Berkshire          Surrey    Kent
              Somerset            Hampshire              Sussex
    Devon           Dorset
                                   Isle of Wight
Cornwall

16

Studies of Surname distribution (for example, *The Movement of British Settlers into Ulster During the Seventeenth Century* by W A Macafee, published in Familia, Ulster Historical Foundation, Belfast, Volume 2, Number 8, 1992 and *The Ulster Plantation* by Philip Robinson, published in The Shaping of the Ulster Landscape by Federation of Ulster Local Studies, Volume 11, Number 2, Winter 1989) tend to support the view that the evolution of predominantly English or Scottish settlement areas in Ulster was established from the earliest days of the 17th century Plantation of Ulster. These studies also show, as evidenced by marked changes in the actual individual surnames at any location between the 1631 muster rolls and 1666 hearth money rolls, that from the earliest days of the Plantation there was a high level of internal mobility and population turnover. Although this internal migration didn't alter the continuity of either English or Scottish predominance it does make the task of identifying the Ulster origins of 17th century British settlers almost impossible owing to the virtual non-existence of 17th century church registers.

Londonderry, Coleraine, Carrickfergus, Belfast and Donaghadee were the main ports of entry into the province of Ulster for 17th century British settlers with the Lagan, Bann and the Foyle valleys acting as the major arteries along which the colonists travelled into the interior. English colonists tended to enter the province along the Belfast-Lagan corridor and the Scots along the Foyle and Bann valleys. As a consequence the southern half of the province tended to be dominated by English colonists with the Scots more prominent in the northern half.

In *The Colonisation of the Maghera Region of South Derry during the Seventeenth and Eighteenth Centuries* (published in Ulster Folklore, Volume 23, 1977) W Macafee investigated Protestant settlement in south Derry by examining surname distribution over time. The sources examined included: 1659 census;1663 hearth money rolls; 1740 religious census returns and the 1831 census. His research showed that after 1700 Protestant settlement in Ulster was formed by internal movements of population rather than by further immigration from England or Scotland. He also concluded that the tenurial framework (based on the townland) established in the 17th century when land was relatively plentiful established areas of Planter/Irish settlement that generally survive to this day. Macafee's research demonstrated that if a townland didn't have a relatively large number of British settlers in occupation by 1740 it never became dominated by them as the native Irish were then able to establish themselves.

John Oliver in tracing his family history (in *Some Ulster Scots and Their Origins in Scotland*, published in Familia, Ulster Historical Foundation, Belfast, Volume 2, Number 3, 1987) plotted the areas in southern Scotland where his family and neighbourhood surnames of the Limavady/Magilligan area (County Londonderry) predominated. He hypothesised that the origins of his Oliver ancestry, which settled in the Limavady area sometime in the 17th century, was the Borders of Scotland, centred on Jedburgh, while Mid-Ayrshire, and in particular the area around Ayr, Irvine and Kilmarnock, was the ancestral homeland of his Magilligan family name of Sherrard. Clearly analysis of surname distribution can provide some useful insight into family origins. It must be stated, however, that only detailed family history research can prove or disprove such theories. As the earliest church registers in the Limavady area, for example, don't predate 1730 it will almost certainly mean there will be insufficient evidence to confirm the exact nature of the link between 17th century Olivers in the Borders of Scotland and those in Limavady. Scottish migration to Ulster had virtually stopped by 1715.

Brian Turner (in *An Observation on Settler Names in Fermanagh*, published in Familia, Ulster Historical Foundation, Belfast, Volume 2, Number 8, 1992) observed that the five most numerous names in County Fermanagh are Maguire, Johnston, Armstrong, McManus and Elliott. Three of these names - Armstrong, Elliott and Johnston - are settler names. Indeed the home of these clans was centred on Liddesdale in the Borders of Scotland. These Border families were well suited to life in the frontier of the Plantation of Ulster. They were a resilient people who stayed in the county throughout the upheavals of the 17th century. The Scots were hardier than the English settlers, and the Borderers were even better adapted again to life on a new, insecure frontier. They had long learnt the art of survival.

I live in the village of Eglinton which is located in the civil parish of Faughanvale, some 10 miles east of the city of Derry. By the 1830s the population of Faughanvale parish was composed of nearly equal numbers of indigenous Irish and immigrant Scots. The roots of these two traditions, Gaelic Irish and Lowland Scottish, were firmly embedded in this parish. Despite the poor condition of the majority of their tenants, the Grocers' Company, in 1822, noted the tenants' "enthusiastic attachment to the residence" of their fathers. They would "submit to any privation rather than quit".

Large-scale emigration since the 1830s, together with the post-war influx of new inhabitants to Eglinton, have, to a large extent, masked the original settlement character of the area.

An examination of the surnames listed in the 1831 census, together with those in even earlier record sources, provides much useful information on settlement patterns laid down before, during and after the 17th century Plantation.

An analysis of the top 80 or so surnames in the parish of Faughanvale in 1831, together with their country of origin, is listed below.

Many of the Gaelic Irish names found in Faughanvale Parish originate in County Donegal, and Inishowen in particular. The predominant Irish Surnames in this parish are evidence of the initial settlement in this area by the expanding Cenel Eoghain (the race of Eogain) from the 10th century, and of later migration of Donegal names into the area just prior to or during the early years of the Plantation.

Most of the major surnames in Faughanvale Parish which were introduced with the 17th century Plantation are of Lowland Scottish origin. Although the names identified in the 1831 census, as being the major surnames of Scottish origin in this area, can be found throughout Scotland (as evidenced by an examination of Scottish telephone directories) they are most heavily concentrated in Southwest Scotland, the Clyde Valley and Clyde Coast, with the heaviest concentration in the Clyde Coast.

# THE TOP SURNAMES IN FAUGHANVALE PARISH

| *Surnames of Irish Origin* | | *Surnames of Scottish Origin* | |
|---|---|---|---|
| Mullen | 38 | Craig | 15 |
| Doherty | 33 | Ross | 15 |
| McLaughlin | 33 | Jameson | 11 |
| Kelly | 27 | Morrison | 10 |
| McGuinness | 21 | Caldwell | 9 |
| McKinney | 19 | Cochrane | 9 |
| McCloskey | 16 | Gilliland | 9 |
| Duddy | 15 | Hannah | 9 |
| Kane | 15 | McNeil | 9 |
| Coyle | 14 | Moore | 9 |
| Donaghy | 14 | Inch | 8 |
| McGonagle | 13 | McCallion | 8 |
| McKeever | 13 | Nelson | 8 |
| Hegarty | 12 | Armstrong | 7 |
| Duffy | 11 | Cowan | 7 |
| Brolly | 10 | Guthrie | 7 |
| Devenny | 10 | Miller | 7 |
| McDaid | 9 | Robinson | 7 |
| McDermot | 9 | Smith | 7 |
| O'Hara | 9 | Stewart | 7 |
| Begley | 8 | Biggart | 6 |
| Devin | 8 | Burns | 6 |
| Gallagher | 8 | Gilfilland | 6 |
| Logue | 8 | Gillespie | 6 |
| Patton | 7 | Henry | 6 |
| Toner | 7 | King | 6 |
| Heany | 6 | Kitchen | 6 |
| McNerlin | 6 | Tedlie | 6 |
| McTaggart | 6 | Archibald | 5 |
| Bradley | 5 | Davis | 5 |
| Feeny | 5 | McFarland | 5 |
| Quinn | 5 | Mackey | 5 |
| Farren | 4 | Morrow | 5 |
| Lynch | 4 | Parkhill | 5 |
| McMenemy | 4 | Scoby | 5 |
| | | Thompson | 5 |
| | | Williams | 5 |
| | | Cunningham | 4 |
| | | Dunlop | 4 |
| | | Dunn | 4 |
| | | Hamilton | 4 |
| | | Major | 4 |
| | | Murray | 4 |
| | | Patterson | 4 |
| | | Proctor | 4 |
| | | Scott | 4 |
| | | Young | 4 |

Key:
38 = Number of households
in the 1831 Census

**Source: 1831 Census**

The lands along the Firth of Clyde in the old county of Ayrshire, stretching from Largs in the north through Ardrossan, Irvine, Kilmarnock, Troon, Ayr, Turnberry, Girvan and Ballantrae in the south, are the homeland of many who settled in Faughanvale Parish in the 17th century. The Clyde Valley and the Border lands (old counties of Wigtown, Kirkcudbright and Dumfries), known today as Dumfries and Galloway, stretching from Langholm in the west through Dumfries, Kirkcudbright, Wigtown, Newtonstewart and Stranraer in the east, would also have provided some of the settlers in the parish of Faughanvale.

The importance of the study of surname distribution in migration research is not just confined to analysing population and family movements within the British Isles. The maintenance of kinship ties is a common thread running throughout 300 years of consistent emigration from Ireland. Indeed kinship ties were often seen as the only redeeming feature of 19th century Ireland by many immigrants to the US and Canada. There were many instances of close and enduring ties between particular localities in the New World and identifiable parishes and even townlands in Ireland. James McGregor, Presbyterian minister of Aghadowey Meeting house, County Londonderry, together with 16 families from his congregation, settled on April 11, 1719 in a township, granted by the Governor of Massachusetts. They called the town Londonderry (New Hampshire).

Based on the 1851 census for New Brunswick, Canada Peter Toner has produced settlement distribution maps for Irish immigrants according to source region in Ireland (*The Green Fields of Canada, Irish Immigration and New Brunswick Settlement 1815-1850*, leaflet produced by the Provincial Archives of New Brunswick, 1991). It clearly demonstrates that Irish immigrants settled near others from the same areas in Ireland. The Irish from eastern Ulster settled in large numbers in Charlotte County while those from Counties Derry, Donegal, Fermanagh and Tyrone (who made up 43% of Irish immigrants to New Brunswick in the period 1815-1850) settled in the entire lower valley of the St John River. Immigrants from the south-eastern corner of Ireland settled in the Miramichi while those from Cork (who provided 19% of Irish immigrants in the period) predominated in the town of St John itself.

Bruce Elliott in *Irish Migrants in the Canadas A New Approach* (McGill-Queen's University Press, Kingston and Montreal, 1988) traced the movements of 775 Protestant families from North Tipperary to the London and Ottawa districts of Upper Canada (ie Ontario) in the period 1815-1855. He found that the location of distant kin was more important than soil fertility, nearness of markets and transportation routes in determining a potential immigrant's choice of destination. Migration was largely a family affair. People moved in families, moved with kin and moved to join kin. Elliott has shown that the locations of family members who had gone before was the major determinant of emigrant destination.

To conclude the study of surnames and of surname distribution, which is fascinating in its own right, can provide clues and insights into the origins of ones family history.

### The Importance of Place in Family History

The key to unlocking your family history origins is a knowledge of place. Movies such as *The Field* or *Far and Away* demonstrate quite forcibly an Irishman's attachment to the land. In rural Ireland today place and kin hold a very strong emotional bond. It is said that when Amelia Earhart (the first woman to fly solo across the Atlantic from Harbour Grace, Newfoundland to Londonderry) landed, on Saturday 21 May 1932, in front of Dan McCallion's cottage, she asked: "Where am I?" An astonished Dan McCallion, who was out herding his cattle, replied: "In Gallagher's Pasture".

Four verses from a poem written by Dave McMurdie of Regina, Saskatchewan in 1943 and dedicated to his old friend Dave Robinson of Vancouver sum up powerfully the strong pull of the Old Country to first-generation immigrants. It is clear that the friendships and places associated with his youth in Bellaghy, County Londonderry sustained Dave McMurdie:

THE OLD HOME TOWN
By Dave McMurdie

It's hard to live on these Prairies Dave, with its terrible frost and snow,
and it's might hard to stick it out where the Northern Blizzards blow.
But the old blood still is in me and I laugh at the Blizzards frown, for
I'm a County Derry man from old Bellaghy Town.

Oh, it's old Bellaghy Town Dave, of its scenes I love to tell,
Palmers Hill, The Shilling Hill and its famous Jean Bells Well.
The Barrack Hall and old stair head to memory I recall,
King William Street I'll ne're forget, nor the dear old Orange Hall.

There were McIntyres and Martins, Millikens and Brown, Mawhineys and
McMurdies always at their post were found, Porters too from Old Drumlamph
and the loyal Bruces too, the loyal Blairs from Mullaghboy and those
Kennedy lads so true.

Oh I know I would die happy Dave, if I once more could roam, through those
lovely scenes and valleys green where once we called our home.
To stand once more by the old Orange Hall, it would fill my heart with
joy to live those old times over again like when you and I were Boys.

The presence of Irish place names in USA, Canada, Australia and New Zealand denote the strength of Irish settlement. There are at least six Londonderrys outside the British Isles: in Canada in the provinces of New Brunswick and Nova Scotia; in USA in the states of New Hampshire and Vermont; In Australia at Cape Londonderry; and in Chile at Londonderry Island.

James McGregor, a gunner on the roof of St Columb's Cathedral during the famous Siege of Derry and Presbyterian minister of Aghadowey Meeting house, County Londonderry, together with 16 families from his congregation, settled on 11 April

1719 in a township, granted by the Governor of Massachusetts. They called the town Londonderry (New Hampshire).

In the Spring of 1818 a group of families arrived at the port of St John, New Brunswick from Londonderry. They may have been disbanded soldiers from a regiment which fought at Waterloo. Forty miles from St John, in the upper reaches of the River St John, they established the township of Londonderry. By the 1920s the settlement was deserted as most of the families had moved on from this relatively infertile area. In the 1950s descendants of settlers at Londonderry got together to renovate the church. Today an annual memorial service is held at St Paul's, Londonderry, New Brunswick to commemorate the original settlers.

The surnames of these settlers are those of the Scottish planters who settled in the Foyle valley, through the port of Londonderry, in the 17th century - Alexander, Anderson, Armstrong, Ashe, Black, Crawford, Crowe, Douglas, Dysart, Ferguson, Forsythe, Hunter, Marshall, McDonald, McFarland, Scott and Williams.

In 1991 when I was travelling on the road to Joseph MacDonald's farm outside Bathurst, New Brunswick it was easy to demonstrate that the Irish are the largest ethnic group in this province (in the period 1815-1850, 70% of immigrants to New Brunswick were Irish). Every twist and turn on the road seemed to have a local name that denoted Irish settlement, with names such as Kelly's Hill, Murphy's Turn (indeed descendants of the original Murphy settler still live there) and Hegarty's Turn.

Place in Ireland has a history stretching back thousands of years. In Ireland clan histories are associated with particular locations (see chapter on The Importance of Surnames in Family History). Surnames are a major component of Irish place names. The following examples of parish names in County Derry (see map of civil parishes on page 26) give some idea of the history that can be contained within a place name:

BALLYSCULLION, meaning "The Townland of O Scollain". The O'Scullions were the erenaghs (hereditary tenants) of the church lands which lay between Bellaghy and Lough Beg. Scullion is still the number one surname in this parish today.

CLONDERMOT, meaning "The territory of the Clan Diarmata (Dermot)". Tracing their lineage from Eoghan, son of the 5th century Niall of the Nine Hostages, Clan Dermot's family name was anglicised to O'Carolan and Carlin. The townland name, in this parish, of Lismacarol, meaning "fort of the sons of Carol" is evidence of their former base. In the 13th century Clan Dermot were overrun by the O'Kanes.

DESERTLYN, meaning "The hermitage of O Floinn". The O'Lynns (also known as O'Flynn) possessed a territory in southern Armagh between Lough Neagh and the sea. They gave their name to the Barony of Loughinsholin, "the lake of the islands of O'Lynn". In the 12th century the O'Lynns were overrun by the O'Kanes.

DESERTOGHILL, meaning "The hermitage of the O Tuathail". The location of this County Derry sept, anglicised Tohill, is indicated by this parish name.

KILCRONAGHAN, meaning "The church of St Cronaghan". St Cronaghan was the teacher of St Columba who founded a monastery at Derry in 546 AD. The ancient church of St Cronaghan was in the townland of Mormeal.

MAGILLIGAN, meaning "The land of Mac Giollagain". This leading north Derry sept of McGilligan were the hereditary tenants (erenaghs) of the churchlands here. In the 17th century the Magilligans were one of the chief septs under the O'Kanes.

TAMLAGHT O'CRILLY, meaning "The burial mound of the O'Crillys". The O'Crillys were hereditary tenants (erenaghs) of the church lands of Tamlaght. This sept originated in the ancient kingdom of Oriel which comprised Counties Armagh and Monaghan.

It is a strong driving force among most people tracing their family history to identify an ancestral home. In Ireland this in effect means identifying the townland your ancestor lived in. The townland is the smallest and most ancient of Irish land divisions, and its identification is essential to researchers who wish to pinpoint the precise origin of their ancestors. There are 60,462 townlands in Ireland.

For practical genealogical purposes Ireland is subdivided into counties which in turn are subdivided into parishes which in turn are subdivided into townlands. As a general rule the knowledge of the county of origin of your ancestor is insufficient evidence for locating them. The Irish Genealogical Project, through computerisation of the major sources and its network of county-based centres, will change this. Ireland is subdivided into 32 counties (see map of Ireland showing counties).

From the seventeenth century the so-called civil parish, based on the early Christian and medieval monastic and church settlements, was used extensively in various surveys. There are 2,508 civil parishes in Ireland. Civil parishes frequently break both barony and county boundaries indicating they were drawn up at an earlier period. Church of Ireland parishes normally conform to the Civil parish, though Roman Catholic parishes do not, as they are generally larger. The Roman Catholic Church, owing to the Reformation of the sixteenth century, had to adapt itself to a new structure centred on towns and villages. County Londonderry, for example, is subdivided into 46 civil parishes (see maps of County Londonderry showing topography and civil parishes). Many records of genealogical value were compiled by civil parish. In many cases, therefore, effective genealogical research requires knowledge of the civil parish in which your ancestor lived.

The townland was named at an early period, and it usually referred to a very identifiable landmark in the local area such as a mountain, a bog, an oak forest, a village, a fort or a church. The townland became standardised as a basic division in the seventeenth-century surveys by people with little knowledge of the Irish language. As a consequence many place names were either lost or had their meaning or construction altered.

# IRELAND

## COUNTY MAP

**IRELAND**

BOUNDARIES

------- Northern Ireland

——— Provinces

——— Counties

Donegal

Londonderry

Antrim

ULSTER

Tyrone

Down

Fermanagh

Armagh

Monaghan

Sligo

Leitrim

Cavan

Louth

Mayo

Roscommon

Longford

Meath

CONNAUGHT

Westmeath

Galway

LEINSTER

Offaly (Kings)

Dublin

Kildare

Leix
(Queens)

Wicklow

Clare

Carlow

Tipperary

Kilkenny

Limerick

Wexford

MUNSTER

Waterford

Kerry

Cork

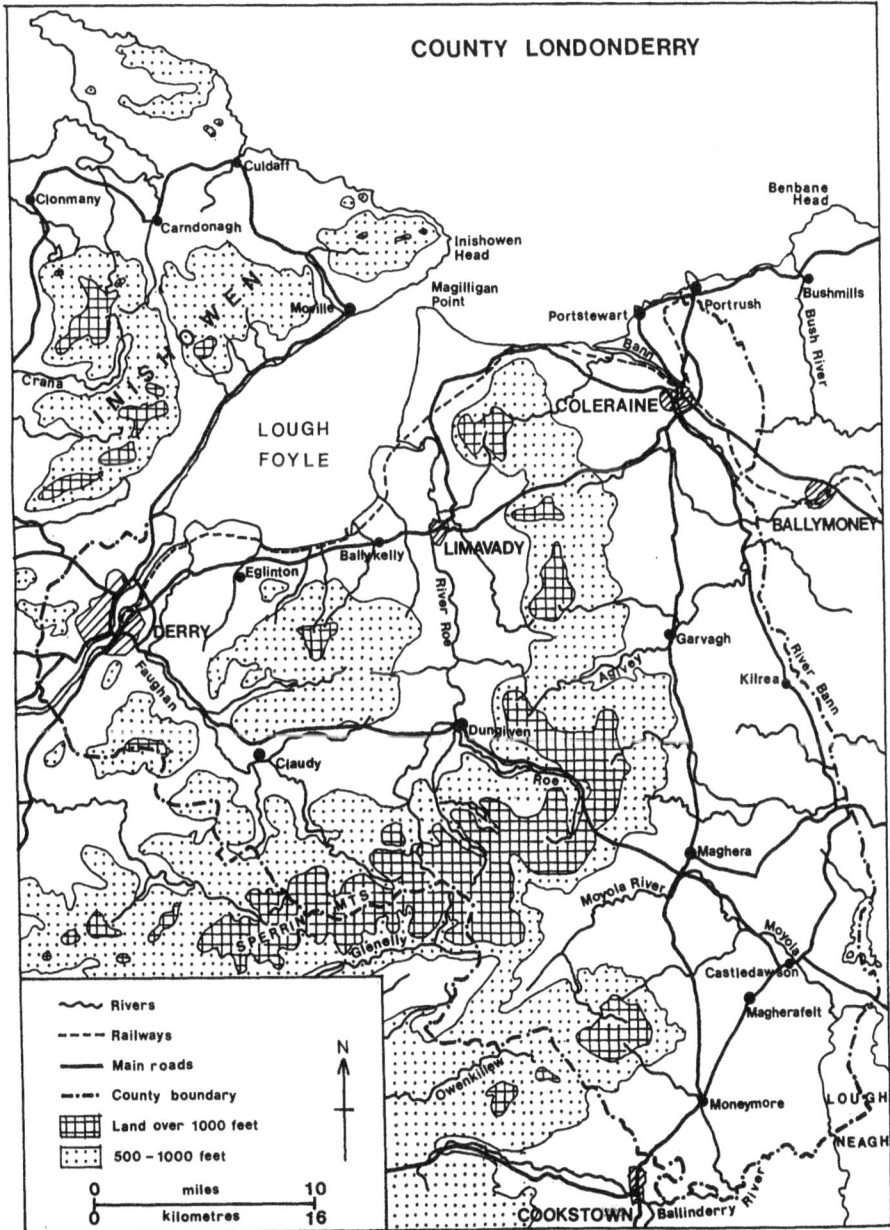

COUNTY LONDONDERRY

Benbane Head
Culdaff
Clonmany
Carndonagh
Inishowen Head
Magilligan Point
Bushmills
Portstewart
Portrush
Bush River
Moville
Bann
INISHOWEN
Crana
LOUGH FOYLE
COLERAINE
BALLYMONEY
Eglinton
Ballykelly
LIMAVADY
River Roe
DERRY
Garvagh
River Bann
Kilrea
Faughan
Agivey
Dungiven
Claudy
Roe
Maghera
Moyola River
Moyola
SPERRIN MTS
Glenelly
Castledawson
Magherafelt
Owenkillew
LOUGH NEAGH
Moneymore
COOKSTOWN
Ballinderry River

Rivers
Railways
Main roads
County boundary
Land over 1000 feet
500 – 1000 feet

N

0 miles 10
0 kilometres 16

25

# COUNTY LONDONDERRY

## CIVIL PARISHES

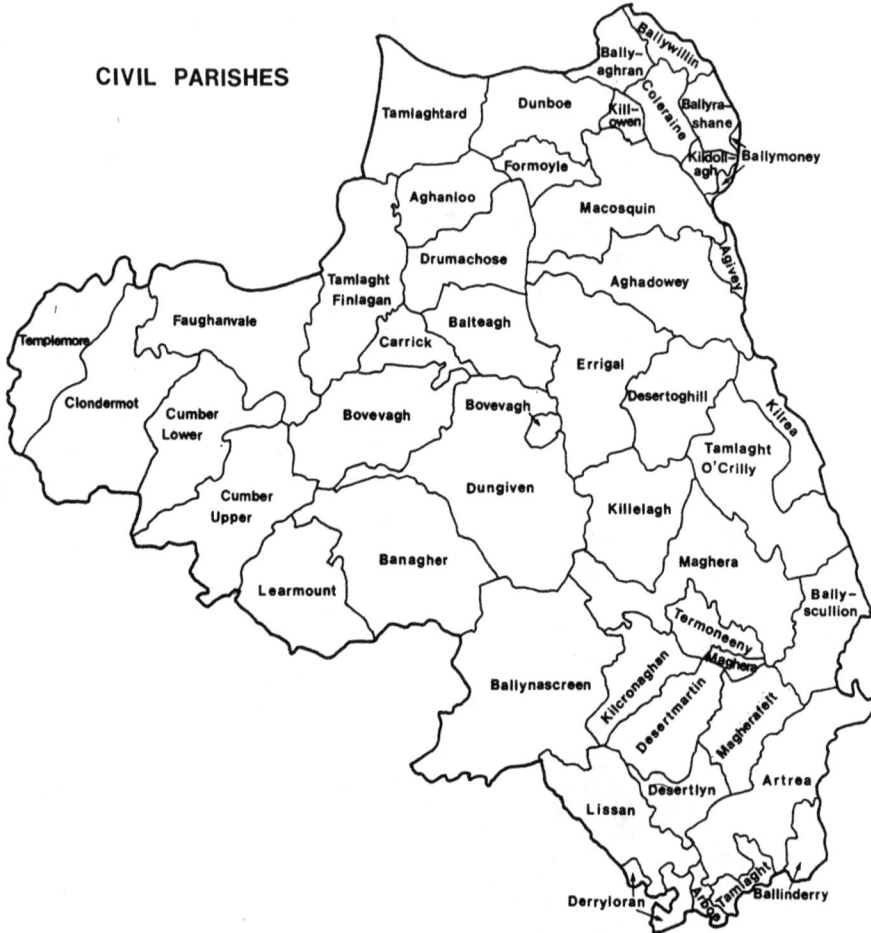

**CIVIL PARISHES**

Ballywillin

Bally-aghran

Coleraine

Killowen

Ballyra-shane

Tamlaghtard

Dunboe

Kildoll-agh

Ballymoney

Formoyle

Aghanloo

Macosquin

Drumachose

Tamlaght Finlagan

Aghadowey

Faughanvale

Balteagh

Carrick

Errigal

Agivey

Templemore

Desertoghill

Kilrea

Clondermot

Bovevagh

Bovevagh

Cumber Lower

Tamlaght O'Crilly

Cumber Upper

Dungiven

Killelagh

Maghera

Banagher

Bally-scullion

Learmount

Termoneeny

Maghera

Ballynascreen

Kilcronaghan

Desertmartin

Magherafelt

Artrea

Lissan

Desertlyn

Derryloran

Tamlaght

Ballinderry

26

There are 66 townlands, for example, in the parish of Faughanvale, County Londonderry (see maps of Faughanvale Parish showing topography and townlands). These townlands vary greatly in area as their size was generally based on the fertility of the land. The fertile lowland townland of Muff is some 318 acres in size, while Killywool which extends into the Loughermore Hills contains 1,471 acres.

The townland is loosely based on the ancient Irish land measure called the ballyboe, which means cow townland. As a ballyboe was based on the area that could support a fixed number of cattle, it is not surprising that their size varied depending on land quality.

It must also be pointed out that there are many place names in Ireland (some of which appear on maps and others that don't) which are even more localised than a townland name. In 1991 the Federation for Ulster Local Studies published *Every Stoney Acre has a name: a celebration of the Townland in Ulster*. Growing up on a farm in the townland of Mettican Glebe near Garvagh, County Londonderry my wife can vouch for the accuracy of this claim. As a child she played in fields with names such as the Horses Leg, the Brogies, the Park, The Rock and The Holly Bush. You will not find these names on any map. Such names are only known to local people. Dwight Radford and Kyle Betit's article on Irish Place Names and the Immigrant (in *THE IRISH At Home and Abroad*, Vol 5, Number 1, 1988) provides much useful advice on identifying more obscure place names.

Ireland was, therefore, divided into a number of administrative divisions which form the geographical basis for research. Records of value to the family historian were gathered by one or more of these divisions. Townland (in rural areas), street (in towns) or parish are the most useful means of identification. The more precise and localised your knowledge of the address of your ancestor, the better your chances of identifying your ancestor.

*A New Genealogical Atlas of Ireland* (Brian Mitchell, Genealogical Publishing Company, Baltimore, 1986) locates for every county in Ireland the following administrative divisions: baronies, civil parishes, dioceses, poor law unions and probate districts. All main record sources are organised by at least one of these divisions:

The Tithe Books were compiled by civil parish in the period from 1823 to 1837. The Griffith's Valuation, undertaken between 1848 and 1864, was organised by poor law union, barony and parish. The early-Nineteenth century census returns were organised by barony and civil parish, while the first surviving census for all of Ireland, namely that of 1901, was arranged by County and District Electoral Division. Seventeenth Century surveys, such as the Civil Survey of Ireland carried out between 1654 and 1656, were arranged by county, barony and civil parish. Marriage license bonds and wills prior to 1858 were administered by Church of Ireland dioceses. From 1858 wills were proved in probate districts. Knowledge of an ancestor's civil parish address, together with their religious denomination, will provide clues as to the appropriate church registers of baptisms, marriages and burials to search. With the introduction of Civil Registration of births, marriages

# FAUGHANVALE PARISH

## TOPOGRAPHICAL MAP

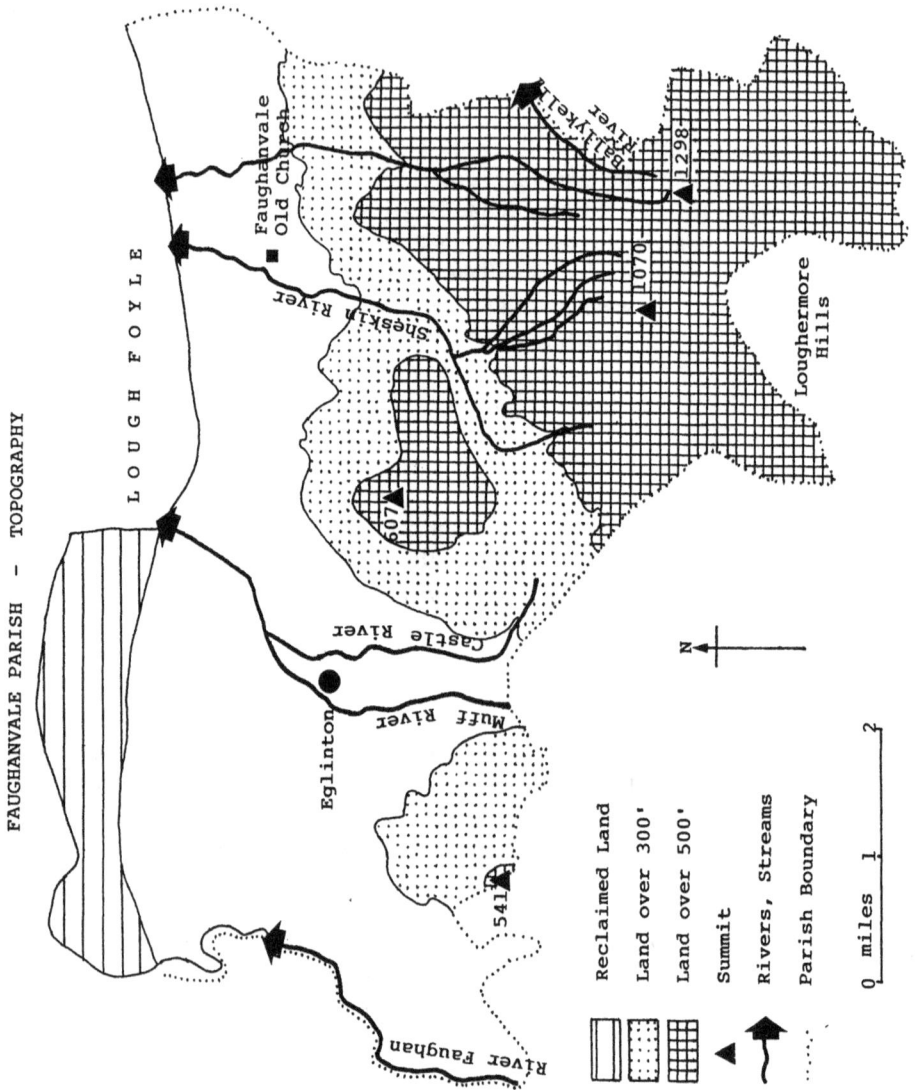

FAUGHANVALE PARISH - TOPOGRAPHY

LOUGH FOYLE

River Faughan

Eglinton

Muff River

Castle River

Sheskin River

Faughanvale Old Church

Ballykelly River

Loughermore Hills

1298

1070

607

541

Reclaimed Land

Land over 300'

Land over 500'

Summit

Rivers, Streams

Parish Boundary

N

0    miles    1    2

# FAUGHANVALE PARISH

## TOWNLANDS

THE TOWNLANDS OF FAUGHANVALE PARISH

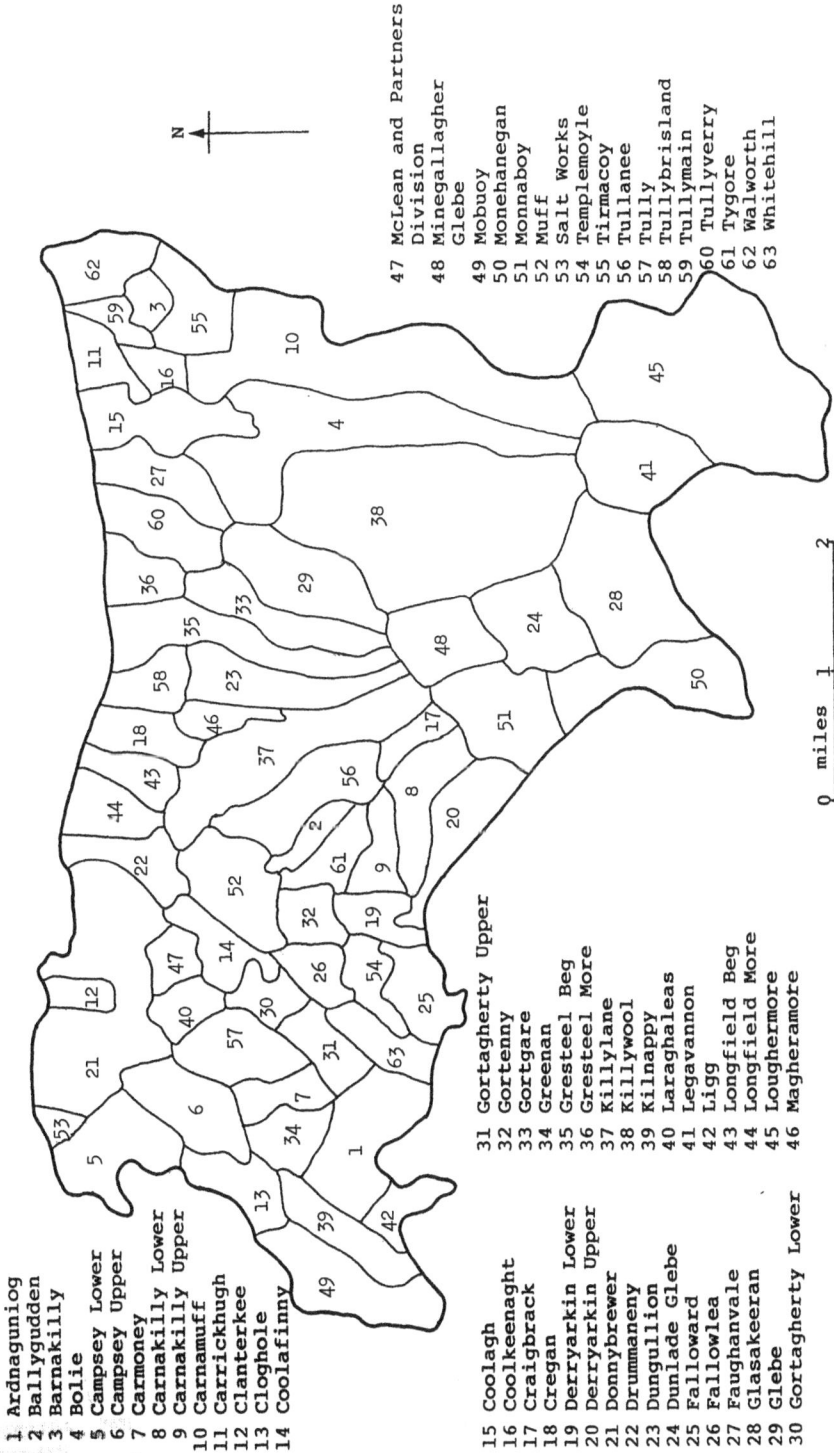

N

0 miles 1 2

1 Ardnaguniog
2 Ballygudden
3 Barnakilly
4 Bolie
5 Campsey Lower
6 Campsey Upper
7 Carmoney
8 Carnakilly Lower
9 Carnakilly Upper
10 Carnamuff
11 Carrickhugh
12 Clanterkee
13 Cloghole
14 Coolafinny

15 Coolagh
16 Coolkeenaght
17 Craigbrack
18 Cregan
19 Derryarkin Lower
20 Derryarkin Upper
21 Donnybrewer
22 Drummaneny
23 Dungullion
24 Dunlade Glebe
25 Falloward
26 Fallowlea
27 Faughanvale
28 Glasakeeran
29 Glebe
30 Gortagherty Lower

31 Gortagherty Upper
32 Gortenny
33 Gortgare
34 Greenan
35 Gresteel Beg
36 Gresteel More
37 Killylane
38 Killywool
39 Kilnappy
40 Laraghaleas
41 Legavannon
42 Ligg
43 Longfield Beg
44 Longfield More
45 Loughermore
46 Magheramore

47 McLean and Partners Division
48 Minegallagher Glebe
49 Mobuoy
50 Monehanegan
51 Monnaboy
52 Muff
53 Salt Works
54 Templemoyle
55 Tirmacoy
56 Tullanee
57 Tully
58 Tullybrisland
59 Tullymain
60 Tullyverry
61 Tygore
62 Walworth
63 Whitehill

29

and deaths the only address information provided in the indexes are the names of the poor law unions in which the events were registered.

I regard the The *General Alphabetical Index to the Townlands and Towns, Parishes and Baronies of Ireland*, better known as the TOWNLAND INDEX (Alexander Thom, Dublin, 1861; reprinted by Genealogical Publishing Company, Baltimore, 1986) as the single most useful reference source in my book collection. For every townland in Ireland this book will identify its civil parish, barony, county, poor law union and District Electoral Division (from 1901) location. This in turn means that you can then figure out what record sources to search for an ancestor who lived in any particular townland.

I would always recommend, as a first step, the identification of civil parish locations associated with your ancestors as this in turn will help determine the selection of appropriate record sources to search. There are a number of reference works, arranged by county and/or record sources, which can then be consulted to identify relevant record sources. Examples include *Irish Genealogy A Record Finder* (edited by Donal Begley, Heraldic Artists, Dublin, 1981), *Irish Records - Sources For Family and Local History* (James Ryan, Ancestry Publishing, Utah, 1988), *A Guide to Irish Parish Registers* (Brian Mitchell, Genealogical Publishing Company, Baltimore, 1988) and *A Guide to Irish Churches and Graveyards* (edited by Brian Mitchell, Genealogical Publishing Company, Baltimore, 1990). The use of these reference works are much more rewarding if you know the parish locations you are interested in.

In the Derry Genealogy Centre we compiled civil parish reports for each civil parish in County Londonderry. The example of Faughanvale Parish is used here as an illustration. This, in effect, means that on one piece of paper we have all the information we need to carry out a search assessment for those people whose ancestors resided in the civil parish of Faughanvale.

In the period prior to 1830 and the work of the Ordnance Survey there was no standardisation in the spelling of townland names. This may mean that the townland name you are looking for is spelt differently to that appearing in the TOWNLAND INDEX. Townland names, originally in Gaelic, were anglicised from the 17th century, by settlers with no knowledge of the Irish language. For example in Clondermot Parish, County Londonderry, the same townland appears as Coolkeeagh in the Griffith's Valuation of 1858, as Killkeeraugh in the 1831 census and as Culkeeragh in the Tithe Book of 1834. Today townland names are spelt on maps the way they were recorded on the mid-19th century Griffith's Valuation. In using the TOWNLAND INDEX, therefore, you should always be aware of potential variant spellings of a place name.

Care must always be taken when interpreting Irish place names in record sources. For example in the passenger lists recorded in the Hardwicke Papers for the years 1803 to 1806 (see chapter on *Emigration and Irish Passenger Lists*) Drumarra refers to Dromara, County Down; NewtownLimavady is better known today as Limavady, County Londonderry; Lowtherstown as Irvinestown, County

# The Townland Index

The *General Alphabetical Index to the Townlands and Towns, Parishes and Baronies of Ireland*, better known as the TOWNLAND INDEX, identifies all of Ireland's 60,462 townlands.

It lists the following information against **each townland**:

1.  An **Ordnance Survey reference number** to the map or maps on which the townland can be located. A record of townland names, shapes and sizes for all Ireland exist in the maps of the Ordnance Survey, completed in 1846, at the scale of six inches to one mile. Once a townland is located on a map it can be located on the ground.

2.  The **size**, in acres, of each townland.

3.  The **County** in which the townland is located.

4.  The **barony** in which the townland is located. Baronies (now an obsolete division) became established in government land surveys of the 17th century.

5.  The **civil parish** in which the townland is located. Many records of genealogical value such as the Griffith's Valuation, Tithe Applotment books, 1831 census, 18th century religious census returns and Flax Growers' Lists were compiled by civil parish. In the absence of indexes, realistic access to these sources requires knowledge of the civil parish in which your ancestor lived.

6.  The **poor law union** in which the townland is located. The poor law union became the basis of the **Superintendent Registrar's District**. The only clue to address in the indexes to Irish civil birth, marriage and death registers is the Superintendent Registrar's District (ie poor law union) in which the event was registered. In 1898 the poor law union replaced the civil parish as the basis of local government administration.

7.  The **District Electoral Division** (from 1901) in which the townland is located. The 1901 census is collated by groups of townlands within their appropriate District Electoral Division.

8.  The **County District** (from 1901) in which the townland is located. Consisting of a group of District Electoral Divisions, each county district had a separate council.

The Townland Index to the 1851 census (which was originally published in Dublin) was reprinted by the Genealogical Publishing Company, Baltimore in 1986.

# Faughanvale Civil Parish

## Parish Report

| | |
|---|---|
| County: | Londonderry |
| Barony: | Tirkeeran |
| Diocese: | Derry |
| Poor Law Union: | Londonderry and NewtownLimavady |
| Probate District: | Londonderry |
| | |
| Area: | 20,496 acres |
| Population in 1831: | 6,218 |
| Topography: | Bounded on the north by Lough Foyle this fertile parish lies 8 miles southeast of the city of Londonderry. |
| Villages: | Faughanvale and Muff (renamed Eglinton in 1858) |
| Landowners in 1837: | The Grocers' and Fishmongers' Companies |

RECORD SOURCES:

| | |
|---|---|
| Tithe: | 1835 |
| Griffith's Valuation: | 1858 |
| Census: | 1663 (Hearth Money Rolls) |
| | 1740 (Protestant Householders) |
| | 1796 (Flax Growers' Lists) |
| | 1803 (Private census by Rev. Elias Thackeray) |
| | 1831 (lists heads of household only) |
| | 1901 and 1911 (lists all family members) |

CHURCH RECORDS:

| | |
|---|---|
| Church of Ireland: | Baptisms, marriages and burials from 1802 |
| Presbyterian: | Baptisms from 1819 and marriages from 1845 |
| Roman Catholic: | Baptisms from 1863 and marriages from 1860 |

GRAVEYARDS AND TOWNLANDS WHERE FOUND

| | |
|---|---|
| Church of Ireland: | Muff |
| Presbyterian: | Tullanee |
| Roman Catholic: | Faughanvale |

TOP TEN SURNAMES IN 1858 (in descending order):

Doherty, McLoughlin, Mullen, Donaghy, Logue, Craig, Duddy, Hara, Kane and McGuinness.

Fermanagh; Queen's County refers to the present-day county of Leix and King's County to Offaly. You should always remember that standardisation in the spelling of both surnames and place names in Ireland is only a phenomenon of the 20th century. In some cases local knowledge within a specific district in Ireland may well be needed to decipher place names. In most cases, however, common sense and a good reference book will be all the assistance required in identifying place names.

In 1847 when the Marchioness of Clydesdale sailed out of Derry port for St John, New Brunswick it was carrying 85 people from Carn. The TOWNLAND INDEX records 29 Carns in Ireland. In this instance, however, Carn refers to the village of Carndonagh in the parish of Donagh, County Donegal. In the northwest, local people will frequently refer to Carndonagh as Carn. Around the town of Garvagh, County Londonderry local people will refer to the parish of Desertoghill as Desert. This can cause confusion as there is a townland called Disert in another County Derry parish, namely Ballynascreen.

I remember someone from Scotland ringing me before planning a trip to Ireland. A marriage certificate in their possession recorded the place of residence of the groom as Coole. The TOWNLAND INDEX recorded 21 townlands called Coole in Ireland and one town of this name (in County Westmeath). The marriage had taken place in Macosquin Presbyterian Church, outside Coleraine in County Londonderry. As marriages tended to involve local people I suspected that the groom was probably from the Macosquin area. The TOWNLAND INDEX confirmed that there were no townlands called Coole in County Londonderry. There was, however, a townland called Coole in the parish of Derrykeighan, County Antrim about 10 miles to the east of Macosquin Presbyterian Church. Furthermore, an examination of the 1:50,000 Ordnance Survey map for Coleraine recorded the place name of Lower Coole Glebe on the banks of the River Bann about 2 miles east of Macosquin Presbyterian Church. A further examination of the TOWNLAND INDEX recorded the townlands of Coole Glebe Lower and Coole Glebe Upper in the civil parish of Macosquin. I, therefore, recommended that research in the first instance should be concentrated on the civil parish of Macosquin. If this produced no results then research could be extended to include the civil parish of Derrykeighan, County Antrim.

Finally, maps were compiled to accompany the Griffith's Valuation. This means that the locations of all properties in the mid-19th century - houses and farms - can be identified once you have found your ancestor in the actual Griffith's Valuation. In other words with these maps you can identify with accuracy the location of the ancestral home (even if it is now long gone) or farm. Householders with no land (such as agricultural labourers or town dwellers) are also identified on the Griffith's Valuation maps.

Every lot number in the Griffith's Valuation (recorded under the heading "No. and Letters of Reference to Map") was marked on a copy of the Ordnance Survey map (at a scale of 6" to 1 mile) at the Valuation Office, Dublin.

Copies of the Griffith's Valuation maps for the 26 counties of Ireland can be found in the Valuation Office, Irish Life Centre, Abbey Street Lower, Dublin while those for the 6 counties of Northern Ireland are held in the Public Record Office of Northern Ireland, 66 Balmoral Avenue, Belfast.

To sum up, once you know the parish and/or townland your ancestor originated from it gives you access to a whole range of genealogical sources. Confirmation, furthermore, of a townland address will enable you to visit the ancestral homeland, talk to local people and perhaps even identify a family homestead. I also believe that a combination of common sense, good maps and the TOWNLAND INDEX will provide answers to most of your place name queries.

# Emigration and Irish Passenger Lists

The story of emigration from Ireland to North America is one of the most fascinating and significant aspects of Irish history of the past three centuries. Irish immigration, furthermore, has played a crucial role in the development of the United States and Canada. Scholarly books such as *The Irish Diaspora A Primer* (by Donald Harman Akenson, published by The Institute of Irish Studies, Belfast, 1996); *Ulster Emigration to Colonial America 1718-1775* (by R J Dickson, published by Ulster Historical Foundation, Belfast, 1988); and *Irish Emigration 1801-1921* (by David Fitzpatrick, published by The Economic and Social History Society of Ireland, 1985) provide much fascinating insight into the process of emigration from Ireland. This insight, not only is it fascinating in its own right (the stuff of Hollywood epics), can assist the family historian in understanding why their ancestor emigrated, how they left Ireland and why they chose where they settled in the New World. Patterns can be identified which might be of assistance in tracking down an individual's family history.

Between 1717 and the War of American Independence, 250,000 Ulster-Scots (ie Protestant settlers in the nine counties of the Province of Ulster) left Ulster, through the ports of Belfast, Londonderry, Newry, Larne and Portrush, for the British Colonies in North America. These Ulster-Scots tended to enter America through Philadelphia and they headed for the frontier. They poured across the Susquehanna into the Cumberland Valley. From the 1740s they moved southwards through the Great Valley, east of the Appalachian Mountains, across the Potomac and into the Shenandoah Valley (also known as the Valley of Virginia) between the Blue Ridge and Appalachian ranges. From there they continued south into the Piedmont of North and South Carolina. By the Revolutionary War, in 1776, about 90% of Ulster settlers had made their homes in Pennsylvania, the Valley of Virginia and the Carolinas; and they dominated a one thousand mile frontier along the spine of Appalachia from Pennsylvania to South Carolina. It was said of the early settlers in Pennsylvania that the Quakers were better traders, the Germans better farmers and the Ulster-Scots were best at coping with frontier conditions. In the words of one Colonial administrator the Ulster-Scots were "troublesome settlers to the Government and hard neighbours to the Indians".

The Ulster-Scots adapted to their new frontier surroundings and quickly declared their allegiance to an independent America. Stories about their families were centred on the frontier not their Ulster origins. They tended not to retain the sentimental ties to their ancestral homeland that became associated with the post-Famine Catholic-Irish emigrant.

With the War of American Independence over the Ulster-Scots then spearheaded the first thrusts across the Appalachian range, through the Cumberland Gap, into Kentucky and Tennessee. By 1792, 100,000 people had moved into the frontier lands through the Cumberland Gap along the Wilderness Road. It was Tennesseans, Kentuckians and Virginians, who ultimately were of Ulster origin, who defended the Alamo in 1836 when Texans rebelled against Mexico.

In the US today an estimated 40 million people claim Irish extraction; 56% of Americans with Irish roots are of Protestant stock, whose roots in many cases can be traced back to the Ulster-Scots who settled on the frontier in the 18th century.

The end of the Napoleonic wars in 1815 is seen as another significant landmark in the story of Irish emigration. From 1815 to 1845 it is estimated that 1 million Irishmen and women crossed the Atlantic for North America. In this period Canada, not the USA, was the initial destination of these emigrants. It is estimated that 80% of passengers who sailed to North America from Irish ports landed in Canada, though perhaps half that total may have gone on to the United States. Prior to the Famine the cheapest way to get to the US was by way of Canada through St John's, Newfoundland, St John, New Brunswick or Quebec.

In contrast to the United States the greatest numbers of Irish came to Canada in the pre-Famine period. By 1871 the Irish-born and their descendants made up 24.3% of Canada's population. In the same year the provinces of Ontario and New Brunswick, with 35% of their population of Irish origin, were the two demographically most Irish jurisdictions outside of Ireland.

In this pre-Famine migration to both the United States and Canada, Protestant Irish migrants continued to significantly outnumber Catholic Irish immigrants. As a consequence, in 1871, 60% of the Irish in Ontario, Quebec, Nova Scotia and New Brunswick were Protestant. The Irish in Canada were, furthermore, rural settlers.

Another feature of this pre-Famine migration is that it affected all parts of Ireland; 18th century emigration had been largely confined to Ulster.

Bruce Elliott (in *Irish Migrants in the Canadas A New Approach*, published by The Institute of Irish Studies, Belfast, 1988) traced the movements of 775 Protestant families from North Tipperary to the districts of London and Ottawa in Upper Canada (ie Ontario) in the period 1815-1855. Elliott concluded that although the decision to emigrate was influenced by economic and social conditions at home, the locations of family members who had gone before was the major determinant of destination.

An examination of the list of emigrants recorded in the Ordnance Survey memoirs for Tamlaght Finlagan Parish, County Londonderry (Royal Irish Academy, Box 47/I/6, pp4-11) records that of the 209 emigrants who left this parish in 1833 and 1834, 151, or 72%, were Presbyterian. It, furthermore, shows that the majority of emigrants travelled in some form of kinship group. In this period 170 people (81%) emigrated from Tamlaght Finlagan Parish in 43 family groupings, ranging from two brothers to a family unit of husband, wife and seven children.

With the depressed conditions following the end of war in 1815 many small farmers and rural tradesmen in Ireland saw emigration as the only solution to their declining economic prospects. In the absence of alternative sources of employment, and in a time of rising population, it was clear that subdivision of the family farm among children inevitably led to deteriorating standards of living. Farms which had

# List of Emigrants from Tamlaght Finlagan Parish in the years 1833 to 1834
## Source: Ordnance Survey Memoirs
### (Courtesy of the Royal Irish Academy, Dublin)

325

County - Derry                    P.h Tamlaght Finlagan

List of Persons who have Emigrated from the
Parish of Tamlaght Finlagan

"P." stands for Presbyterian —
R.C. for Roman Catholic
E.C. for Established Church —

| Name | Age | The year in which the Persons left the Country | Townland in which the Person Resided | Religion | Port to where Emigrated |
|---|---|---|---|---|---|
| William M°Clane | 22 | 34 | Ballymore | P | ... |
| David Work | 20 | 34 | do | P | ... York |
| James Baird | 58 | 33 | do | P | Philadelphia |
| William Baird | 28 | 33 | do | P | Philadelphia |
| James Baird jun° | 23 | 33 | do | P | do do |
| Robert Baird | 18 | 33 | do | P | do do |
| John Baird | 9 | 33 | do | P | do do |
| Ann Baird | 30 | 33 | do | P | do do |
| Elenor Baird | 27 | 33 | do | P | do do |
| Maryann Baird | 14 | 33 | do | P | do do |
| Martha Baird | 7 | 33 | do | P | do do |
| John M°Conlis | 25 | 33 | do | P | do do |
| John Stewart | 48 | 34 | do | P | do do |
| Jane Stewart | 40 | 34 | do | P | do do |
| William Stewart | 16 | 34 | do | P | do do |
| John Stewart | 14 | 34 | do | P | do do |
| Robert Stewart | 12 | 34 | do | P | do do |
| Hugh Stewart | 1 | 34 | do | P | do do |
| Jane Stewart | 10 | 34 | do | P | do do |
| Elizabeth Stewart | 8 | 34 | do | P | do do |
| Maryann Stewart | 6 | 34 | do | P | do do |
| Andrew Morrison | 22 | 34 | Moys | P | do |
| Joseph M°Cracken | 20 | 34 | do | P | do |
| James Neiley | 25 | 33 | do | P | do |
| Joseph Neiley | 23 | 33 | do | P | Philadelphia |

BOX 47 I 6          25 May 1834 Thomas Fagan

37

been leased to one tenant in the 1780s were by the 1820s, in many cases, being sub-let to three, four or five families. To prevent subdivision the only solution seemed to be to send surplus sons to North America.

The Great Famine resulted in unparalleled emigration. Between 1846 and 1851 over a million people left Ireland for North America. From the 1830s the port of Liverpool emerged as the preferred port of embarkation for Irish emigrants. By the Famine the Liverpool-New York route was the main artery of Irish emigration. New York received about 67% of the total number of Irish who emigrated to the US between 1848 and 1851. In the same period nearly 74% of Irish emigrants departed from Liverpool with Irish ports carrying only 20% of Famine emigrants.

In Ireland the potential emigrant was most likely to be a farm labourer: in the USA the Irish immigrant's principal role was to service industrial expansion.

There is a tendency to see the Famine as the cause of the Irish Diaspora. In reality heavy emigration from Ireland began well before the Famine and continued well after it. Between 1856 and 1914 some 4 million people emigrated from Ireland. The Famine speeded up events that were already in evidence. In the 19th century and early-20th century the economic and social corner-stone of Irish society was the family-operated farm. In 1851, 83% of the Irish population lived in the countryside with tenant farmers' families accounting for over half of the rural population, and the families of landless labourers the bulk of the remainder. As subdivision of the family plot was no longer seen as a viable economic solution (from well before Famine times) it effectively meant that surplus sons and daughters of tenant farmers had to migrate in search of marriage and employment opportunities. In the post-Famine period David Fitzpatrick noted that only about one-third of the typical family of six children could hope to inherit or marry into land.

Another aspect of change that had begun before the Famine was termed by David Fitzpatrick as a "class collapse". In the fifty years after the Famine male farm workers, previously the largest group employed in Ireland, declined dramatically in number. Landless labourers declined sharply from over 700,000 in 1851 to just under 260,000 in 1901. Emigration was in these circumstances the only opportunity on offer in Ireland. Emigration thus acted as a "safety valve", enabling frustrated young men and women with little economic prospects to escape Ireland.

In the period 1850 to 1914 the majority of Irish emigrants went to the USA and they were Catholic. Beginning in the late 1820s relatively poor Catholics from the three southern provinces of Ireland (ie Connaught, Munster and Leinster) constituted a major proportion of the movement overseas.

Alone among major European countries, women left Ireland in numbers approaching those of males. Between 1800 and 1922 about 4 million females emigrated from Ireland. In rural Ireland it was quite often the case that a woman unable or unwilling to enter a marriage with a man who was to inherit the family farm would chose to emigrate. Most emigrants were under 25 years of age. In any one year less than 20% of emigrants from Ireland were over 30 years old.

From its earliest days Irish migration has been a family affair. The Irish either moved with kin or moved to join kin. Indeed kinship ties were often seen as the only redeeming feature of 19th century Ireland.

After the Famine emigrant streams from Ireland were dominated by lone emigrants, usually young and unskilled. They nevertheless moved along kinship pathways. This trend was noted in the Ordnance Survey memoirs of the 1830s. The Ordnance Survey memoir of Clondermot Parish (Royal Irish Academy, Box 34/I/24 pp54-55) noted: "In most cases from one to three of the youngest, strongest and healthiest of a family, without distinction of sex, emigrate together and send for the older members the following season under favourable circumstances....Two thirds had the expenses of their passage defrayed by earlier emigrants...The few who furnish their entire passage money themselves are only respectable farmers, or individuals from whose families no emigration has yet been made".

The 19th century emigrant trade depended to a large extent on people in North America paying the fare to bring out family and friends. The selection of future emigrants, therefore, lay largely with those who had gone before. Once emigration from a neighbourhood began it tended to be sustained by this chain mechanism.

Thomas Mullen of Wilmington, Delaware, for example, paid the fare for one James Mullen at the Philadelphia office of Andrew J Catherwood on 6 January 1853 (Public Record Office of Northern Ireland, reference T2002/1). The certificate issued entitled James Mullen to steerage passage, from Derry to Philadelphia, on any ship of the Derry company, J & J Cooke. James Mullen from Plumbridge, County Tyrone made use of this certificate to emigrate on the ship *Superior* in the spring voyage of 1853 (Public Record Office of Northern Ireland, Ref: MIC 13).

As I stated earlier I believe that some understanding of the process of emigration to North America can provide some assistance in tracing the Irish origins of immigrants. The next issue which needs to be addressed is the extent to which either North American arrival records or Irish Passenger Lists can assist you in tracing the actual origins of your Irish family history.

I suspect that Australia alone among the nations to which Irish migrants moved in significant numbers has records of individual migrants that permit the tracing of large numbers to their precise home backgrounds in Ireland. This was because most 19th century emigration to Australia was assisted by government and they kept very good records. For example the passenger arrival record for the ship *Africana* in Sydney, New South Wales in March 1866 records the following information about John Callaghan and his wife Bridget:

| Name | Age | Residence | Parents and their Residence | Religion |
|------|-----|-----------|----------------------------|----------|
| Callaghan John | 38 | Coolcross Co Donegal | Owen and Susan living at Coolcross | RC |
| Callaghan Bridget | 37 | Clonmany Co Donegal | Michael & Bridget Doherty, both dead | RC |

Occupations and the names of any relatives in New South Wales are also recorded as well as the names and ages of John and Bridget Callaghan's children. Clearly a complete family tree can be compiled with this one piece of information.

As the keeping of "official" passenger lists began in 1855 in Canada it means that Canadian arrival registers will be of little value to most Canadians tracing their Irish roots. Most Irish immigrants arrived in Canada prior to 1855. Bruce Elliott advocates a genealogical approach to studying emigration patterns in Canada as there are virtually no passenger lists for the pre-1855 period when Irish emigration to Canada was most intensive. Researchers must build up their own list of immigrants from a region from detailed genealogical study and comparison of Irish and Canadian sources such as parish registers, census returns, land records and gravestone inscriptions.

One hundred and seventy eight passenger lists compiled by the authorities in British and Irish ports and presented to Custom House officials' in New Brunswick ports have survived for the years, 1833, 1834, 1837 and 1838 (published in *Passengers to New Brunswick The Custom House Records - 1833, 34, 37 & 38* by New Brunswick Genealogical Society, Saint John Branch, 1987). The majority of these lists give details as to name, occupation, place of origin and age. As many people from the Northwest of Ireland emigrated through St John, New Brunswick in this time period these lists could be of great value. Thirty passenger lists from the port of Derry, for example, survive in these Custom House records of St John, New Brunswick.

From 1820, the United States required ships' captains to lodge lists of passengers arriving at American ports with the collectors of customs. These customs passenger lists provide only two clues relating to the origin of the emigrants: the port of departure of the ship and the nationality of the passenger. Specific information regarding the emigrant's place of residence was not given. From a genealogical point of view this information is of little value. The Irish port of departure of an emigrant does provide a slight clue to an ancestor's origin. For example, it is fair to assume that an ancestor who emigrated through the port of Derry had their origins in either Counties Derry, Donegal or Tyrone. It must also be remembered that from the middle years of the 19th century onwards most Irish emigrants left from Liverpool, thus providing no clues as to their place of origin (even a general one) in Ireland.

It wasn't until the passing of the Immigration Act of 1893 that it became compulsory for masters of vessels to record the former residence of passengers. This essentially means that US arrival records are of limited genealogical (but of great sentimental value) value prior to 1893. The so-called "Old Immigration" of peoples from northwestern Europe (ie Ireland, Britain and Germany) had by then passed its peak. It is the peoples of the "New Immigration" which began in the 1880s, who came from southern European countries, namely Greece, Italy and Russia, who will dominate the Immigration Passenger Lists. Of course many of the 16 million immigrants who passed through Ellis Island, the principal immigrant receiving station, from 1892 to 1954 will be Irish.

A query about the availability of passenger lists in Ireland is by far the most frequently asked question by visitors to the Derry Genealogy Centre. The only comprehensive and complete recording of passengers departing from Ireland are the Board of Trade Passenger Lists (Public Record Office, Kew, Surrey, England, BT27). These lists, arranged by year and ship's name under the ports of departure, detail passengers leaving the United Kingdom of Great Britain and Ireland (Northern Ireland, after 1922) by sea between 1890 and 1960. The name, age and occupation of each passenger is given. It wasn't until 1922 that these forms asked for the last place of residence of British emigrants. Lists earlier than 1890 no longer exist. With Board of Trade records only occasionally providing a place of residence of Irish emigrants prior to 1922 these lists will be of limited genealogical value.

The only official registers of passengers leaving Irish ports which survive prior to 1890 were those kept for a brief period from March 1803 to March 1806 inclusive. For this brief period lists of emigrants to the United States are contained within the so-called Hardwicke Papers. These lists with particulars of age, occupation and, in most cases, place of abode were compiled by masters of emigrant ships and were sworn before the Commissioner, a Customs Official, in the Custom House of the port of embarkation.

A duplicate of these oaths were then submitted to the Lord Lieutenant of Ireland. The Lord Lieutenant's permission was required before an emigrant ship could leave an Irish port. Earl Hardwicke was Lord Lieutenant of Ireland from 1801 to 1806. The majority of sailings recorded in the Hardwicke Papers (the original papers are held in the British Museum) were from the ports of Dublin (28 sailings), Londonderry (26), Belfast (22), Newry (19) and Sligo (6). The information from the Hardwicke Papers was published in *Irish Passenger Lists 1803-1806* (edited by Brian Mitchell, Genealogical Publishing Company, Baltimore, 1995).

If your ancestors emigrated from either Counties Antrim or Londonderry in the 1830s you may indeed be very fortunate. The Ordnance Survey memoirs for Counties Antrim and Londonderry (the original papers are held in the Royal Irish Academy, Dublin) are unique in that for many of their parishes lists of emigrants for a few years in the mid- to late-1830s were compiled. As emigration records these lists are unparalleled (see list of emigrants from Tamlaght Finlagan Parish on page 37). They identify both the destinations of the emigrants and their places of origin in Ireland. In addition to recording the actual townland address of each emigrant the memoirs recorded their age, year of emigration and religious denomination. The usefulness of such information is self-evident. With a name, age, townland address and religious denomination, for example, it should be possible to identify the baptism entry of an ancestor (assuming the baptism registers exist). The emigrant lists from the Ordnance Survey memoirs of Counties Antrim and Londonderry were published in *Irish Emigration Lists 1833-1839* (edited by Brian Mitchell, Genealogical Publishing Company, Baltimore, 1989).

Prior to 1890 surviving passenger lists in Ireland largely owe their existence to ship owners, who kept them for business reasons. The port of Londonderry is especially fortunate in this regard, having two series of such lists - the shipping lists of J & J

Cooke, 1847-1867, and William McCorkell & Co, 1863-1871. These lists generally provide the name, age and address of the passenger with the name of the ship.

In the years 1847 to 1867 J & J Cooke carried 21,199 passengers to North America. In 1847, at the height of the Famine, this company carried 5,071 emigrants (1,197 (23%) to Philadelphia; 2,210 (44%) to St John, New Brunswick and 1,664 (33%) to Quebec).

By the nineteenth century the emigrant trade depended to a large extent on people in North America paying the fare to bring out family and friends. These "engaged" passengers insured the viability of the passenger trade for Londonderry shipping firms in the middle years of the 19th century. For the years 1863 to 1871 the order book of William McCorkell & Co records the names of 5,184 passengers. All these intending emigrants were "engaged" in Philadelphia by Messrs. Robert Taylor & Co.

The original shipping lists of J & J Cooke and of William McCorkell & Co are held in the Public Record Office of Northern Ireland (Microfilm copies of the Cooke lists on MIC13 and of the McCorkell lists on MIC14). These lists were published in *Irish Passenger Lists 1847-1871* (edited by Brian Mitchell, Genealogical Publishing Company, Baltimore, 1988).

One example will suffice to show the potential value of passenger lists which record the emigrant's place of residence.

The Order Book of Londonderry Shipping Company J & J Cooke records that on Tuesday 30 March 1852 Bernard and Biddy (Bridget) Gormley of Claudy booked their passage at a total cost of £7 on the Spring voyage of the J & J Cooke ship, *Mary Ann*, to St John, New Brunswick, Canada. The advertisement for the sailing of this ship is recorded as follows in the *Derry Journal*:

DIRECT FROM DERRY - NOTICE TO PASSENGERS
Those Persons who have taken passage by the Ship
MARY ANN
Captain John Hatrick
FOR ST. JOHN'S, N.B.
Are required to be on board on TUESDAY, the 30th
March as the Vessel will proceed on her voyage
immediately after that date. A few more Passengers can be
taken by this fine ship if immediate application be made
to the Agents in the Country or here to
J & J Cooke. Londonderry, March 9, 1852

*The Maiden City and the The Western Ocean* (by Sholto Cooke and published by Morris and Company, Dublin), which records the history of the Shipping Trade between Londonderry and North America in the 19th century, provides some information about the *Mary Ann*. The *Mary Ann* was bought by the Derry-owned Shipping Company of J & J Cooke in 1851 at a cost of £2,460. Built by David Mundle of Richibucto, New Brunswick she was registered in the port of Derry on

28 February 1851 with the following dimensions: Tonnage 405; length 118.6 feet; beam 24.4 feet; depth 17 feet.

In the period 1851 to 1859, under the captaincy of John Hatrick, the *Mary Ann* was a regular trader to both St John and New Orleans. Her best passage was St John to Derry in 20 days - in those days Derry to St John was the fastest passage between Europe and North America.

Early in April 1852 the *Mary Ann* sailed out of Lough Foyle with her complement of 196 passengers drawn from Counties Derry, Donegal, Fermanagh and Tyrone. An examination of the order book of J & J Cooke confirms that Derry served as an emigration port for counties Donegal, Derry and Tyrone. Of 1,395 passengers carried on Cooke ships in 1850, 553, or 40%, came from County Donegal; 363, or 26%, from County Tyrone; and 307, or 22%, from County Derry, ie 88% of all passengers carried came from these three counties. Eighty-six, or 6%, came from County Fermanagh, while twenty-six, or 2%, came from County Antrim. Monaghan, Leitrim and Roscommon made up the rest (see map of the catchment area of the port of Derry).

In the Ship's order book Bernard and Biddy Gormley's address was recorded as Claudy which is a small village some 7 miles southeast of the city of Derry on the banks of the River Faughan. This would suggest that the ancestral homeland of Bernard and Bridget Gormley was the farmlands surrounding the village of Claudy.

The implications for the family historian are clear. As Claudy is located in the civil parish of Cumber Upper it means ancestral research, in the first instance, should be concentrated on sources in this parish:

CUMBER UPPER CIVIL PARISH - RECORD SOURCES:

**Church Registers:**

| | |
|---|---|
| Church of Ireland: | Baptisms 1811-1818 and from 1826 |
| | Marriages 1811-1814 and from 1837 |
| Presbyterian: | Cumber Upper - Baptisms and marriages from 1834 |
| Roman Catholic: | Claudy - Baptisms 1853-1854 and from 1863 |
| | Marriages from 1863 |

**Graveyards:**

| | |
|---|---|
| Church or Ireland: | Cumber |
| Roman Catholic: | Village of Claudy |

**Census and Census Substitutes:**

| | |
|---|---|
| Tithe: | 1828 |
| Griffith's Valuation: | 1858 |
| Census: | 1663 (Hearth Money Rolls) |
| | 1740 (Protestant Householders) |

# The Catchment Area of Derry Port
## for the Emigrant Trade to North America in 1850

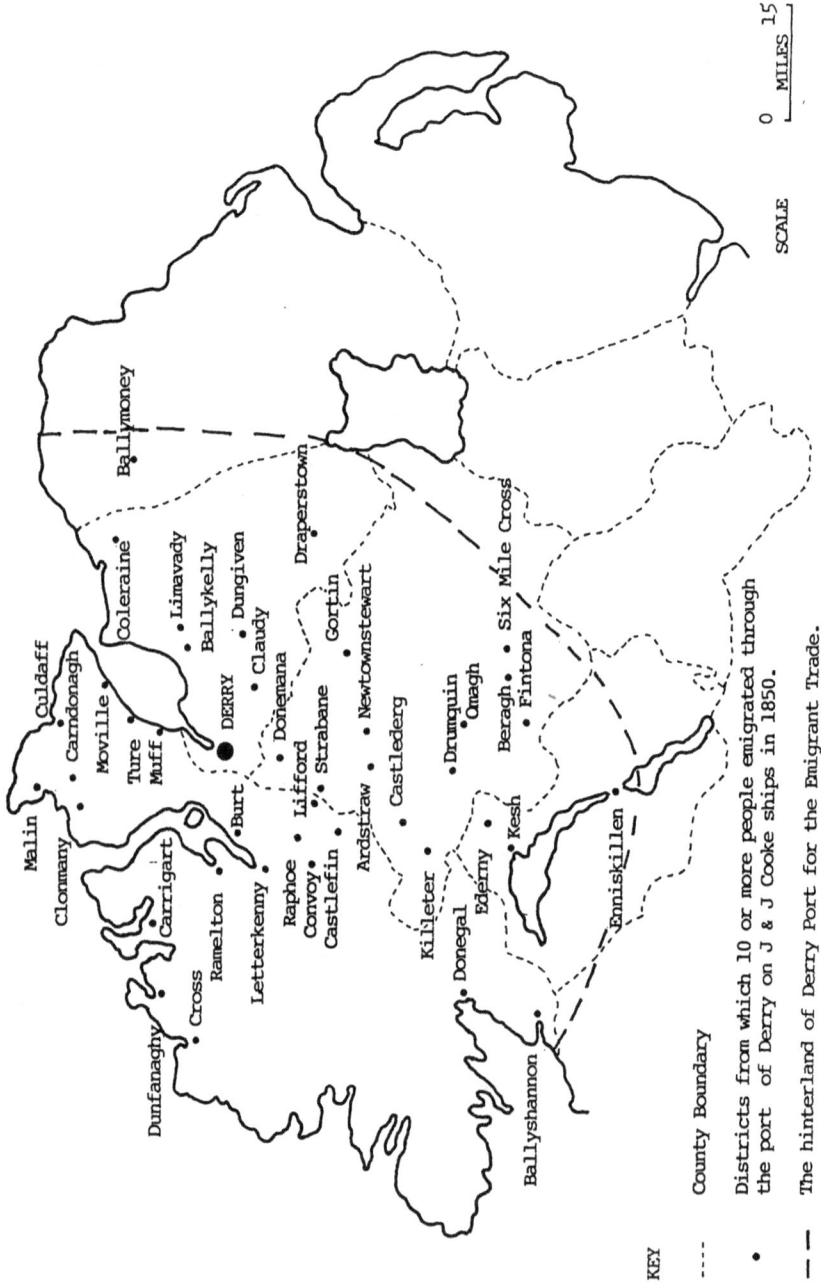

THE CATCHMENT AREA OF DERRY PORT FOR THE EMIGRANT TRADE TO NORTH AMERICA IN 1850

Ballymoney

Draperstown

Coleraine

Limavady

Ballykelly

Dungiven

Claudy

Gortin

Six Mile Cross

Culdaff

Carndonagh

Newtownstewart

Malin

Moville

Ture

DERRY

Donemana

Drumquin

Onagh

Beragh

Fintona

Muff

Lifford

Strabane

Ardstraw

Castlederg

Clonmany

Burt

Carrigart

Raphoe

Castlefin

Convoy

Killeter

Dunfanaghy

Letterkenny

Ramelton

Donegal

Ederny

Kesh

Cross

Enniskillen

Ballyshannon

SCALE

0 ———— 15

MILES

KEY

--- County Boundary

• Districts from which 10 or more people emigrated through
the port of Derry on J & J Cooke ships in 1850.

— The hinterland of Derry Port for the Emigrant Trade.

44

1796 (Flax Growers Lists)
1831 Census (lists heads of household only)
1901 Census (lists all family members)

Two options are, therefore, very feasible. You can either examine all the above sources in the Public Record Office in Belfast or commission the Derry Genealogy Centre, who have indexed all the above sources, to search their database to compile a report on the Gormley family tree. If the above research is negative you could then consider extending your research to the parish of Cumber Lower.

Edward MacLysaght's *Irish Families Their Names, Arms and Origins* (published by Irish Academic Press, Dublin, 1985) also throws insight into the origins of the Gormleys. In the 14th century the O'Gormleys were driven by the O'Donnells from their original territory in the Barony of Raphoe, County Donegal. They then settled on the other side of the River Foyle between Derry and Strabane. Although it is unlikely that record sources will take the actual family history of Bernard Gormley back beyond the early 1800s it is quite plausible that his Gormley ancestry resides in the Claudy area since Medieval times.

Finally, the "American Letter" had an important role to play in the encouragement of the Irish to emigrate. The letter, with details of the voyage and of conditions in their adopted country, would have been read aloud to friends and to members of the family group. It played its part in changing the Irish attitude to emigration from one of resignation to one of acceptance and, even of, anticipation. These letters provide a fascinating insight into the nature of emigration. The Thompson family of Londonderry, for example, still retain letters, dating from the 1860s, that were sent to the ancestral home in Articlave, County Londonderry by various Thompson immigrants in Philadelphia, Cincinnati and Brooklyn, New York Just imagine if all the address information in such letters, at either end of the migration path, were centrally documented what a picture of transatlantic migration they would paint.

## Using Record Sources in the US and Canada to identify your Irish Ancestor

It is not my intention to provide an in-depth analysis of sources and record offices in the US and Canada of value to the family historian seeking clues to the origins of his/her Irish ancestry. Indeed it would be presumptuous of me to do so. I have spent 20 years researching sources in Ireland and four hours in the United States! Instead I will use examples drawn from my own experiences of how information provided from sources in North America have assisted people trace their Irish roots. Many of these examples are drawn from County Derry - the oakleaf county. In the past decade, as manager of the Derry Genealogy Centre, we have assisted some 5000 people trace their roots.

In 1988 I had the privilege of visiting the Family History Library in Salt Lake City. In the space of one evening I managed to identify three generations of family detail on the Metcalf branch of my family tree from Headington in Oxfordshire. In four hours I managed to examine the parish registers of Headington Parish Church, the 1841 census, the index to civil birth registers and the International Genealogical Index. I also left the library that evening with photocopies of relevant details from these sources together with maps and topographical information on Headington. This information was gained at no cost to myself, except for a very nominal charge for the photocopies I made. In addition I was able to select the appropriate reels of microfilm to view and to photocopy without having to complete any form filling or seek staff permission..

So my first piece of advice to anyone tracing their roots is quite simply to make use of the impressive network of Family History Libraries established by the Mormons. If my memory serves me well two floors of their vast library in Salt Lake City was devoted to sources in the United States and Canada, one floor to the British Isles (ie Ireland, England, Scotland and Wales) and one floor to Europe and elsewhere.

For those of Irish descent in Canada and the USA the tracing of your Irish roots doesn't begin in Ireland. It begins in your home country. It is only by building up a picture of your ancestors in their adopted country will you find the necessary clues to make a worthwhile search in Ireland. You should attempt to establish the following information:
- Where was the original emigrant from, preferably the townland or parish address
- What was his or her religious denomination
- What are the ancestor's vital statistics, ie dates of birth, marriage and death
- When did your ancestor emigrate

In some cases family tradition may be able to provide this information, but in most cases various records will have to be searched for this information. Your aim should be to extract information against three key words: NAME, LOCATION and DATE.

Irish Family History Research begins with your surname (see chapter on *The Importance of Surnames in Family History*). The only tangible link that many people of Irish descent in Canada and the US retain with Ireland is their family name. Your surname can provide clues and insights into the origins of ones family history. I would always recommend an examination of surname reference books to find out as much as you can about the origins of surnames in your family tree. Irish surnames, whether of Gaelic-Irish or of Scottish and English origin, frequently provide clues to a place of origin, as many names have a territorial basis.

It is fair to say that the more common your surname is in Ireland the more precise your knowledge needs to be of where your ancestor originated. For example you could not justify a genealogical search for the surname McMahon if all you know is that they originated in County Clare. This is because, at the time of the mid-19th century Griffith's Valuation, there were 661 McMahon households in this county. On the other hand you could justify a search for the surname Eves in County Fermanagh, as in the middle years of the 19th century, there were only two households bearing this surname in the county.

It would seem appropriate at this point to mention the publication of a CD-ROM index to the mid-19th century Griffith's Valuation for every county in Ireland in a joint initiative by the Genealogical Publishing Company of Baltimore, Broderbund Software and Heritage World of County Tyrone, Ireland. This index offers the researcher the ability to quickly search for the townland/street address of a named ancestor. The value of such a source is self-evident as the Griffith's Valuation recorded all heads of household in mid-19th century Ireland. Although there have been reservations raised about the level of mistakes and omissions I still believe this source will provide many people in the US and Canada with the key to unlocking their Irish roots. If this index identifies the townland address of your ancestor it effectively means that you can, if you wish, visit the ancestral homeland. The task of identifying appropriate church and civil records to search is, furthermore, quite straightforward if you know the townland your ancestor lived in.

As effective genealogical research in Ireland requires knowledge of the civil parish in which your ancestor lived all references to place in your family history should be carefully recorded. Many records of genealogical value were compiled by civil parish (See chapter on *The Importance of Place in Family History*).

The more precise and localised your knowledge of the address of your ancestor, the better your chances of identifying your ancestor. Townland (in rural areas), street (in towns) or parish are the most useful means of identification.

In the period prior to 1830 and the work of the Ordnance Survey there was no standardisation in the spelling of townland names. This may mean that the place information you hold is spelt differently to that appearing in a modern map.

With the advantage of local knowledge we frequently were able to suggest possible locations for place names provided by clients of the Derry Genealogy Centre. For example, in one case, we suspected that Aughadewy referred to Aghadowey (a district and parish in County Derry), and in another that Stradeough was the townland of Stradreagh in the civil parish of Clondermot. In another case family tradition stated the family was baptised in Kilcrimaghan Parish Church, which we suspected was Kilcronaghan Church of Ireland Church.

You should, therefore, always take careful note of any place information. The following extract from one letter to the Derry Genealogy Centre sums up the value of family tradition: "Dad always told me that he remembered hearing that the original family farm was on *the Claudy Road* and as one of the photos has a caption that reads *the original Gilfillan home at Ballynamore, on the Claudy Road, southeast of Londonderry*". This family knowledge provided all the information that we needed to make a successful genealogical search. The Townland Index identified the townland of Ballynamore as being located in the civil parish of Cumber Lower. The 1:50,000 Ordnance Survey map, Sheet 7 for Londonderry, locates the townland of Ballynamore about 4 miles to the northwest of the village of Claudy. A quick examination of the Griffith's Valuation confirmed that Ballynamore was the Gilfillan ancestral homeland. Households headed by Alexander Gilfilland junior, Alexander Gilfilland senior and William Gilfilland were residing and farming here in 1858.

You should always attempt to find out if there are other people researching your ancestor or, even better still, if your family history has been published. I can still remember two visitors to the Derry Genealogy Centre, within days of each other, one from California, the other from South Carolina tracing the same ancestor. They were not aware of each other's interest in the same family history, and their combined knowledge provided much useful insight.

At first glance there seemed to be some discrepancies in the above case; tradition in one family stated that the wife of their ancestor Robert Canning was a Mary Ann Steel and in the other that it was Mary Wilson. Our research suggested that both were right. The Derry Genealogy Centre's database of civil marriage certificates recorded the marriage of Robert Canning, a widower to Mary Wilson in 1857. Although our database didn't record the first marriage of Robert Canning it does seem quite feasible that Mary Ann Steel was Robert Canning's first wife.

In another case we were able to provide the family history of one John Walker who was born in County Tyrone c 1697 without examining a single record source. This was because another American visitor had in her possession a typescript showing the direct descendants of one Thomas Walker, born c. 1538 in Nottinghamshire, England. This Thomas Walker was the great-grandfather of George Walker, Governor during the famous Siege of Derry of 1689.

There are now many genealogical sites on the Internet. David Hawgood author of *Internet for Genealogy* says: "The first thing to do is a search on the genealogy of your own surname. The other thing is to publish your own web pages. If people search for your surname they will find you."

In 1998 The Federation for Ulster Local Studies organised a one-day workshop on "Computers as a gateway to exploring local history". This workshop demonstrated the value of the Internet in "opening up new and sometimes surprising opportunities in local history investigations."

I think it is fair to say that, unfortunately, for many people North American passenger arrival records will be of little assistance in tracing the actual origins of their Irish family history (See chapter on *Emigration and Irish Passenger Lists*). I suspect that Australia alone among the nations to which Irish migrants moved in significant numbers has records of individual migrants that permit the tracing of large numbers to their precise home backgrounds in Ireland. This was because most 19th century emigration to Australia was assisted by government and they kept very good records.

In the US, it wasn't until the passing of the Immigration Act of 1893 that it became compulsory for masters of vessels to record the former residence of passengers. This essentially means that US arrival records are of limited genealogical (but of great sentimental value) value prior to 1893.

In compiling his book detailing the histories of 775 families who migrated from North Tipperary to Ontario, Canada in the period 1815 to 1855 (*Irish Migrants in the Canadas A New Approach*, McGill-Queen's University Press, Kingston and Montreal, 1988) Bruce Elliott noted that "very few lists of emigrants or immigrants survive". As the keeping of "official" passenger lists began in 1855 in Canada it means that Canadian arrival registers will be of little value to most Canadians tracing their Irish roots. Most Irish immigrants arrived in Canada prior to 1855.

Bruce Elliott advocated that "the researcher must therefore build up his own list of immigrants from a region from detailed genealogical study and constant comparison of Irish and Canadian sources". He identified parish registers, census returns, land records and gravestone inscriptions as the most useful genealogical sources in Canada.

I will record here some of Bruce Elliott's conclusions on the value of Canadian sources. He regarded the censuses of 1842, 1852, 1861, 1871, 1881 and 1891 as the most important sources for tracing migrants once they arrived in Canada. Parish registers, especially those of the Church of England were another invaluable source. He noted that a record of baptism was often the first and sometimes the only evidence that a family was in a given community. He also found that gravestones were a much more important source in Canada than they were in Ireland, largely owing to the improved economic circumstances of many emigrants. Finally, land records were useful in determining family relationships and approximating dates of arrival and departure.

Between 1815 and the Canadian Confederation in 1867 more than 150,000 immigrants from Ireland arrived at St John. It is estimated that some 30,000 people (more people than were living in the city at the time) arrived at St John during the Famine years of 1845 to 1847. In such circumstances the New Brunswick census of 1851 is the most important single source for the study of Irish immigration to the province of New Brunswick. In the census of 1851, over half the heads of households in the city of St John, New Brunswick registered themselves as natives of Ireland. Professor Peter Toner of University of New Brunswick, St John published in 1991 *An Index to Irish Immigrants in the New Brunswick Census of 1851*. The end product of his research, which included many case studies, was the identification of the Irish county of origin for some 30% of the immigrants.

Peter Toner noted: "On a very small scale, there are now quite a few studies of specific families on both sides of the Atlantic. Long derided by scholars as "mere genealogy", these studies constitute a collective resource which is rapidly gaining the attention of social historians. After all, enough families taken together make a community, and enough communities can make a nation."

In short it would seem that the world of genealogical research has more to offer the scholarly world of migration studies than vice versa.

There are many sources in North America that can be of assistance in building up clues to the origins of an Irish ancestor. Some time ago I remember reading about a New York genealogist, B-Ann Moorhouse, who made use of federal and state censuses, marriage and death records, naturalization records, directories, passenger lists, probate records, cemetery inscriptions and death notices in newspapers to research 400 Irish-born and their descendants who resided in Brooklyn, New York during the 19th century. Regarding clues to place of origin in Ireland, she found death notices in the local Brooklyn newspapers of the time to be of most value, as they consistently gave the exact place of origin of the Irish-born. In another case, the will of William Ferguson, dated 1873, in mentioning a farm his sister had left to him in Ballygarvey in Rathaspick parish, County Westmeath, identified the Irish origins of this Brooklyn merchant.

The type of information that you may discover, in your searches of North American sources, can be best demonstrated by a few examples. In St Mary's Cemetery in Lee, Massachusetts, the following headstone inscription can be found: "*John Dooley, a native of the town of Leabeg, parish of Ferbane, King's County, died August 14, 1863 aged 53 years.*" King's County is now renamed Offaly. In Barkerville cemetery in Barkerville, British Columbia, one of the tombstones reads: "*In memory of Patrick McKenna, native of Duleek, County Meath, Ireland, died June 2, 1914 aged 59.*" With these two tombstones you have sufficient information to begin a search into the Irish origins of John Dooley and Patrick McKenna. It must be emphasised, however, that there will be many occasions when a tombstone provides no or limited clues to Irish origins. "Native of Ireland", for example, is of little help in tracing your ancestor's Irish origins!

Death notices and obituaries in newspapers should also be sought out. The *Herald*, the local newspaper of Charlottetown, Prince Edward Island, on 3rd July 1867 carried the following death notice: "*On Monday June 3rd at his residence, Monaghan Settlement Lot 36, James Trainor, aged 80 years. The deceased was a native of the parish of Donah, townland of Strawmore, County Monaghan, Ireland and emigrated to this island in the year 1835, May he rest in peace.*"

In the following example the details of two obituaries in local newspapers in Glencoe, USA provided a very full family history of the Hasson family in Ireland, Canada and the US:

Obituary - 1 November 1893
*Died - At his residence in Dodge...Jacob Caldwell Hasson, in the 77th year of his age...Jacob Caldwell Hasson was born in County Derrey, Ireland, Jan 2 1817. He*

*was married to Isabella Rogers in 1847 and moved to Canada in 1848. In 1849 he moved to the United States, settling in New York city. In the year 1871 he moved to Dodge county, Nebraska, and settled near Glencoe. He lived there until 1888 when his wife died...He leaves six children, sixteen grand-children, three great-grand-children and one brother to mourn his loss."*

Obituary - 25 March 1894
*Last Sunday, March 25, Mr William Hasson..after a short illness passed peacefully away. He was born in Bovava, County Londonderry, on March 4, 1811. On the 28 of March 1839, he married Miss Ann Morrison with whom he lived happily for 55 years...In 1842 they removed to New York where they resided for 14 years. From here they removed to Burcan county, Illinois, and for 15 years followed the occupation of farming. In 1871 they removed to Dodge county, Nebraska, and lived on a farm near Glencoe, later moving into Dodge...He was brought up in the Presbyterian Church and early became a member."*

These two obituaries provide ample information to begin searching record sources in Ireland. The placename of Bovava almost certainly refers to the townland and/or civil parish of Bovevagh in County Londonderry. As the Hassons were Presbyterian a natural starting point in researching this family tree would be an examination of the church registers of Bovevagh Presbyterian Church. As the baptism registers of Bovevagh Presbyterian Church don't begin until 1818 we would not expect to find the baptisms of either Jacob or William Hasson, but siblings might be recorded. The graveyards in the Protestant churches of the civil parish of Bovevagh should also be searched for Hasson headstones.

As Protestant marriages were subject to civil registration from 1845 a search should be made for the marriage of Jacob Hasson to Isabella Rogers. If found, the marriage certificate will record the names of the fathers of bride and groom and record the addresses of Jacob Hasson and Isabella Rogers in 1847. In other words it would also provide clues to the ancestral home of the Rogers family.

Searches could be made of the early-19th century Tithe Books, 1831 census, mid-19th century Griffith's Valuation and 1901 census for references to Hasson in the civil parish of Bovevagh.

If the above sources confirm that Hassons have been settled in this parish from the beginning of the 19th century then a search of census records and census substitutes of the 18th century for Bovevagh parish should be carried out. The 1796 Flax Growers Lists, 1766 Religious Census, 1740 Protestant Householders Lists and 1663 Hearth Money Rolls all list heads of household for the civil parish of Bovevagh.

Thus a relatively comprehensive picture of the Hasson family tree in Ireland could be constructed from the information supplied in obituary notices in the US.

Birth, marriage and death certificates can provide useful detail. For example, the birth certificate in the State of Ohio for James Maxwell identified the birthplaces and ages of his parents. Based on the information in this certificate it would seem

51

that James' father, Samuel A Maxwell was born in Cork, Ireland c. 1899 and that his mother, Isabella McKell Kilpatrick was born in Glasgow, Scotland c. 1904. This is sufficient information to justify a search of the civil birth registers of Ireland and Scotland for the births of Samuel A Maxwell and Isabella Kilpatrick respectively.

The death certificate of John Deeney who died in 1926 in the State of New Jersey, for example, provides much useful genealogical information. This certificate records that John Deeney was born on 17 March 1862 and that his parents were Daniel Deeney and Mary Logue. It also records that his wife was Mary Higgins. John Deeney's birthplace and that of his parents were simply recorded as Ireland. As civil registration of births in Ireland didn't begin until 1864 it means that you will have to rely on church baptismal registers to confirm the birth details of John Deeney. Clearly the death certificate on its own provides insufficient information on which to select appropriate church registers to search.

Indeed this example proved the real worth of the databases being created by the network of centres in Ireland as part of the Irish Genealogical Project (see chapter on *Genealogy Centres in Ireland - How to make the best use of them*). A search of the database of pre-1900 Roman Catholic Church registers computerised by the Derry Genealogy Centre recorded the marriage of a Daniel Deeny of Umracam to Mary Logue of Umracam in Feeny Roman Catholic Chapel on 2 November 1851. It would seem that John Deeney was born in the townland of Umrycam in the civil parish of Banagher, County Londonderry.

In Canada, it has been said, that an effective way of linking an ancestor to his place of origin in Ireland is the identification of a marriage entry of a newly-arrived immigrant in a church register. Frequently, these marriage registers give a county of birth in Ireland, and occasionally, the exact place of origin of bride and groom. In the years 1801 to 1845, for example, the marriages of 3,000 Irish immigrants, giving their parents' names and native parishes, were recorded in Halifax, Nova Scotia.

To many Irish immigrants in the US and Canada kinship ties were often seen as the only redeeming feature of 19th century Ireland. In these circumstances it is not surprising that many immigrants were eager for news from relatives in Ireland. In the following letter (recorded in the Ordnance Survey Memoirs for Maghera Parish, County Londonderry) which was sent by a female school teacher in Philadelphia, with the initials M.D., in 1836, to her Uncle, it is clear that she missed the close knit community of friends and relatives in her native Maghera. Her letter finishes "Be pleased to remember me to all my friends present my best compliments to Nelly - to all the children, Mr and Mrs Crilly - Owen McLead and his wife. Remember me to all of the Hagan family to the Thompson family and to every friend who will think it worth while to enquire about me. Give my respects to Mary Laverty and tell her that her two fine boys come to see me every Saturday evening".

Many families still retain letters that were sent to their ancestors from relatives who remained in Ireland. In addition to the wealth of family detail these letters offer they frequently will provide the townland address of the sender. For example the

McClement family of the US were able to identify their ancestral home as the townland of Bratwell, in the civil parish of Dunboe, some 3 miles to the south of the village of Articlave in County Londonderry. This was because they held a copy of a letter, dated 12th December 1933, sent by James Archibald, a cousin. James had clearly recorded his address in full at the top of the letter as Bratwell, Articlave, Co Derry, Ireland. An examination of civil birth registers identified the birth of their ancestor William John McClamond in the townland of Bratwell on 25th January 1871.

In another case, a letter dated January 16 1853 simply recorded the name Gortagerty. An examination of the Townland Index quickly confirmed that this referred to the townland of Gortagherty in the civil parish of Faughanvale, County Londonderry.

Naturalization records are another useful source. When Christopher James Devlin, formerly of Glasgow, Scotland, declared his intention to become a citizen of the United States the form recorded that his wife, Bridget Hendry was born in County Derry, Ireland on 31 October 1855.

In the Naturalization records of Rutland County in the State of Vermont it is recorded that Andrew Graham born in the town of Ballynacross in the County of Londonderry on 11th January 1783 did declare on oath, before the County Court, on the 18th September 1838 his "intention to become a citizen of the United States, and to renounce, forever, all allegiance and fidelity to any foreign prince, potentate, state or sovereignty, whatever, and particularly to Victoria Queen of the United Kingdom of Great Britain and Ireland whereof you are, at present, a subject".

The Townland Index records three townlands called Ballynacross in Ireland, but only one in County Londonderry. It would seem, therefore, that the townland of Ballynacross in the civil parish of Maghera in County Londonderry was the ancestral home of the Grahams. A quick examination of the Griffith's Valuation for Maghera Parish would tend to confirm this as one Robert Graham was farming 20 acres of land in Ballynacross in 1859.

I hope these few examples and anecdotes go someway to illustrating the range of sources out there that might just provide the clue you have been searching for. I realise that I have provided no deep insight into sources and record offices in the US and Canada. There are many fine reference books on North American sources that cover this detail more competently than I could ever hope to achieve. I believe that there is nothing to beat experience when it comes to genealogical research. You can only get a 'feel' for record sources and what they contain by examining them. I certainly feel I've learned as much about record sources from unproductive research as I have from successful research. Persistence, dedication and enthusiasm will often win through.

## How to make the best use of Church Registers

Civil registration of births, deaths and Roman Catholic marriages didn't begin until 1864 in Ireland, though Protestant marriages were subject to registration from April 1845. Before these dates baptism, marriage and burial details of an ancestor will be found in church registers. As birth, marriage and death certificates are indexed on an all-Ireland basis, it is probably fair to say that parish registers lose their importance with the introduction of civil registration. For the first half of the nineteenth century and before, parish registers are an indispensable source of information for the genealogist.

Before seeking out church registers you will need to know in which civil parish your ancestor lived, and their religious denomination - Roman Catholic, Church of Ireland, Presbyterian or other dissenting Protestant.

The organisation of churches in Ireland can cause confusion. The Church of Ireland was able to establish an all-Ireland parish structure because of its privileged position, prior to 1871, as the Established Church. The Church of Ireland parish largely coincides with the boundaries of the civil parish and retains the civil parish name. The church and its parish structure evolved like any other organisation. Throughout the 18th and 19th centuries new parishes were carved out of existing parishes or parishes united to form a new parish. Churches became separated from the old burial places as new churches were constructed. For example, the Old Clondermot Parish Church in County Londonderry was built in the townland of Clondermot in 1622. By the middle of the 18th century this church was falling into disrepair, so a new church was erected on its present site in Altnagelvin townland in 1753. By 1867 the Church of Ireland population of the parish had risen to 1,500. A new parish called All Saints with its church in the townland of Clooney, was separated from Clondermot parish, to accommodate the large number of parishioners living in the Waterside area of the city of Londonderry.

With disestablishment it was deemed that Church of Ireland records of baptism and burials prior to 31 December 1870, and marriages prior to 31 March 1845, should become public records. As a consequence, by 1922, the original records of 1,006 parishes were deposited in the Public Record Office in Dublin while 637 were retained in local custody. With the fire in the Public Record Office in 1922 all but four of the 1,006 registers were burnt. The effect of the fire was more severe on some counties than on others. In County Dublin, with 99 civil parishes, seventy-two pre-1871 church registers survive of which seventeen have commencement dates between 1619 and 1699. In contrast County Kildare, with 110 civil parishes, has only sixteen registers with pre-1871 commencement dates.

Owing to its numerical strength the Roman Catholic church was also able to set up a parish network which included within it every townland in Ireland. This parish network, however, frequently doesn't correspond with either the names or boundaries of the civil parishes. The Penal Laws and the active persecution of Catholics resulted in the late erection of chapels in many parishes and the late commencement of many Catholic registers. Catholic registers, especially in the bigger cities, can be of an early date. There are baptism and marriage records for

Wexford town dating back to 1671. Dublin city has no less than nine parishes with registers commencing before 1800, the earliest being St Michan's, which has baptism and marriage registers dating from 1726. In contrast, the registers of predominately rural counties often start at a late date. Of the forty-one Roman Catholic parishes serving the 52 civil parishes of County Donegal, twenty-nine of them have registers that don't commence until after 1850. Nine of the Catholic parishes have registers with commencement dates in the 1840s, while another two have entries from the 1830s. Only one register, Clonleigh, with entries from 1773, goes back into the eighteenth century. The reason for this is, in part, owing to the actions of an enlightened landlord. The local landlord, the Earl of Erne, conscious that Catholics had to attend Mass in the open air, donated a piece of land at Murlog on which Clonleigh chapel was erected about 1760.

The Presbyterian church doesn't have a parish structure as such, with the congregations generally forming where there was sufficient demand from local Presbyterian families. In those areas with a high Presbyterian population, there could be many Presbyterian meeting houses. For example, the civil parish of Ballymore in County Armagh had six Presbyterian congregations by the middle of the nineteenth century. By contrast, in County Wicklow, with 57 civil parishes, there was only one Presbyterian congregation - at Bray. The other Protestant dissenting denominations, such as Methodists, Baptists, Congregationalists and Quakers, formed where there were enough like-minded people.

It is very noticeable that the Presbyterian congregations in Ireland are very much associated with the nine counties of the northern province of Ulster. One feature of the Presbyterian Church is the concentration of congregations within relatively small areas. Doctrinal differences and disagreement over a choice of a minister often divided the original congregation and led to the creation of a new congregation. One example from County Londonderry demonstrates this process. In 1777 a secession congregation was formed at Crossgar by a party which had separated from the congregation of Macosquin. In 1812 some members of Crossgar objected to how the *Regium Donum*, or King's gift, a payment made to Presbyterian ministers, was to be allocated, so they withdrew and formed a new congregation at Ballylintagh. Ballylintagh in turn split to form a secession church at Dromore.

The difficulty presented by this growth of congregations, largely in Ulster, lies in identifying the correct Presbyterian register to search. You will probably find that two or three registers may have to be searched even if you know the exact area your ancestors lived in. My wife, for example, is descended from at least four generations of Presbyterian farmers in Garvagh, County Londonderry, yet the family's allegiance over the last 150 years has fluctuated between First Garvagh, Second Garvagh and Boveedy Presbyterian churches. Furthermore, some of her Presbyterian ancestors were buried in the original Desertoghill Church of Ireland graveyard.

Religious and civil persecution resulting from the Penal laws may explain why there are few Presbyterian registers going back into the 18th century. Of 68 Presbyterian Congregations in County Londonderry only three have baptism or marriage registers with entries predating 1800, namely Ballykelly, First Garvagh and First Magherafelt.

These differences in the structure of the three major denominations are illustrated for County Londonderry with maps (drawn by my father, Sam Mitchell) showing: civil parishes (which largely match Church of Ireland parish boundaries, see map of civil parishes on page 26); Roman Catholic parishes; and location of Presbyterian churches (within civil parishes).

It is very possible for the baptism, marriage and burial records of Protestant dissenters to be within the registers of the Church of Ireland. For centuries the Established Church claimed the right to administer baptism, marriage and burial ceremonies to all Protestants, regardless of denomination, as the exclusive prerogative of the Church of Ireland clergy. For example, until 1782 marriages between dissenters, celebrated by their ministers, were illegal. Until 1844 a marriage between a dissenter and a member of the Established Church was considered illegal if performed by a dissenting minister. Prior to the Burial Act of 1868, which permitted dissenting ministers to conduct burial services, the Church of Ireland clergy held jurisdiction over funeral services for Protestants. Clearly, if you have Presbyterian, Methodist, Baptist, Congregational or Quaker ancestry, it is essential that you do not overlook the Church of Ireland registers. It is also true that members of the Established Church frequently became dissenters. I have a great-grandfather who was baptised and married Church of Ireland but died a Methodist.

After identifying the religious affiliation of your ancestor and their residence, you need to identify what church registers exist for your area and their dates of commencement. The commencement dates of registers vary from church to church. For example the Church of Ireland register for St Columb's Cathedral, Londonderry dates from 1642 while the earliest Roman Catholic register in County Londonderry doesn't predate 1822.

The absence of relevant records is a well known problem in Irish genealogy as many records were destroyed or simply not recorded until quite late on. If, for example, your County Derry ancestors were Roman Catholic it is highly unlikely, no matter how persistent you are, that you will be able to confirm birth or marriage details of your ancestors prior to 1822.

There are a number of reference works which can be used to assist in identifying church registers and their dates of commencement.

John Grenham in his extremely comprehensive *Tracing Your Irish Ancestors* (second edition, Gill & Macmillan, Dublin, 1999) provides "a listing of all copies of Roman Catholic parish registers, microfilm and database transcript, to be found at present (1998) in the National Library of Ireland, the Public Record Office of Northern Ireland, the LDS Family History Library and local heritage centres, as well as those which have been published." On a county basis John Grenham provides a map showing the Roman Catholic parishes together with a table

# COUNTY LONDONDERRY

# ROMAN CATHOLIC PARISHES

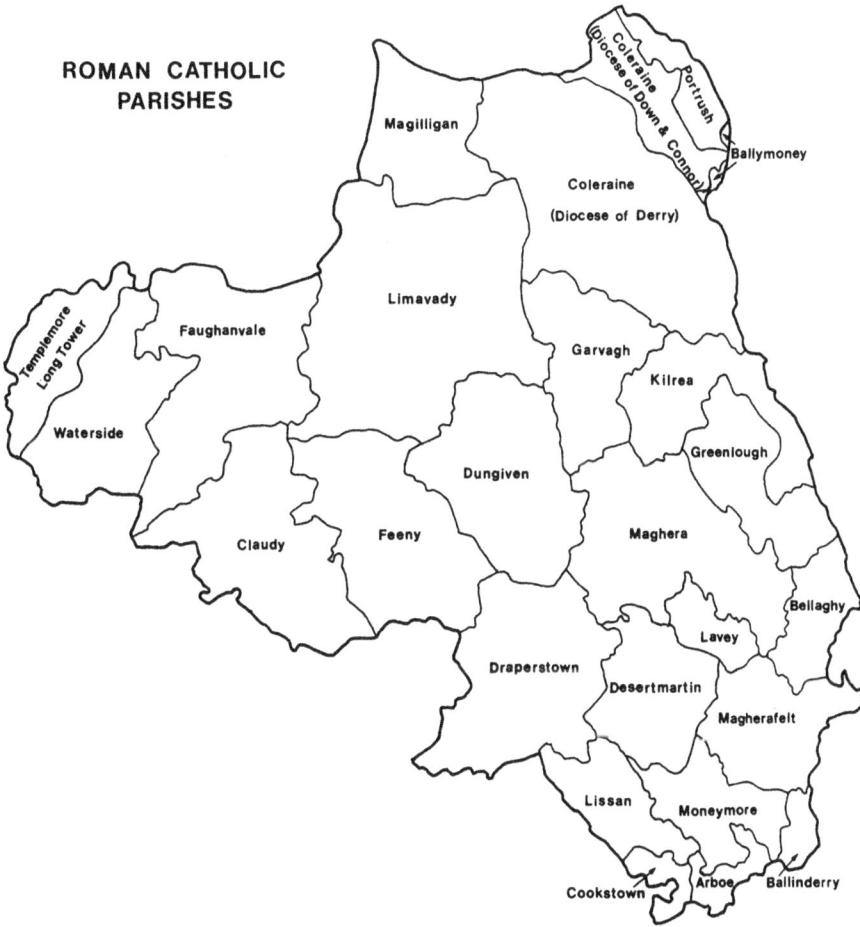

# COUNTY LONDONDERRY

## PRESBYTERIAN CONGREGATIONS

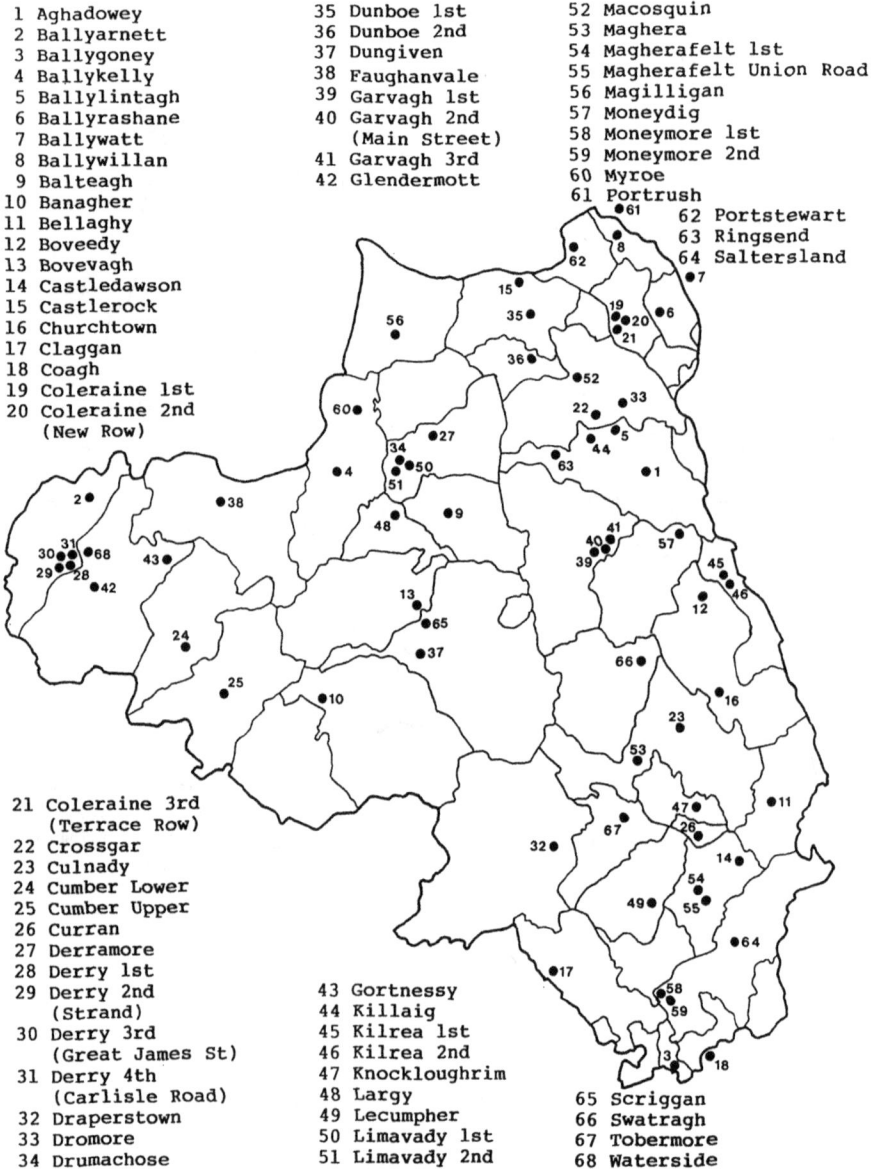

PRESBYTERIAN CONGREGATIONS

1 Aghadowey
2 Ballyarnett
3 Ballygoney
4 Ballykelly
5 Ballylintagh
6 Ballyrashane
7 Ballywatt
8 Ballywillan
9 Balteagh
10 Banagher
11 Bellaghy
12 Boveedy
13 Bovevagh
14 Castledawson
15 Castlerock
16 Churchtown
17 Claggan
18 Coagh
19 Coleraine 1st
20 Coleraine 2nd
   (New Row)

35 Dunboe 1st
36 Dunboe 2nd
37 Dungiven
38 Faughanvale
39 Garvagh 1st
40 Garvagh 2nd
   (Main Street)
41 Garvagh 3rd
42 Glendermott

52 Macosquin
53 Maghera
54 Magherafelt 1st
55 Magherafelt Union Road
56 Magilligan
57 Moneydig
58 Moneymore 1st
59 Moneymore 2nd
60 Myroe
61 Portrush
62 Portstewart
63 Ringsend
64 Saltersland

21 Coleraine 3rd
   (Terrace Row)
22 Crossgar
23 Culnady
24 Cumber Lower
25 Cumber Upper
26 Curran
27 Derramore
28 Derry 1st
29 Derry 2nd
   (Strand)
30 Derry 3rd
   (Great James St)
31 Derry 4th
   (Carlisle Road)
32 Draperstown
33 Dromore
34 Drumachose

43 Gortnessy
44 Killaig
45 Kilrea 1st
46 Kilrea 2nd
47 Knockloughrim
48 Largy
49 Lecumpher
50 Limavady 1st
51 Limavady 2nd

65 Scriggan
66 Swatragh
67 Tobermore
68 Waterside

identifying dates of coverage of baptism, marriage and burial registers of each parish and where copies and indexes of these registers can be found.

The Public Record Office of Northern Ireland is in the process of building up microfilm copy of all church registers of baptisms, marriages and burials (especially for the pre-civil registration period) in the nine counties of Ulster (ie Antrim, Armagh, Cavan, Donegal, Down, Fermanagh, Londonderry, Monaghan and Tyrone). PRONI produced its *Guide To Church Records* (Ulster Historical Foundation, Belfast, 1994) as it recognised that "a major problem in using church records is identifying which records exist in a particular area and for what dates." This book, in alphabetical order by civil parish, records church registers of all denominations and their reference number in PRONI, for the 9 counties of Ulster. In addition to recording dates of coverage of church registers it also notes details of vestry books, session minutes, pew rent books, communicants' rolls etc. The latter sources will often shed light on the important role churches played in the life of the community, particularly in education and welfare.

In *A Guide to Irish Parish Registers* (By Brian Mitchell, Genealogical Publishing Company, Baltimore, 1988) an attempt was made to locate churches of all denominations within their civil parish and provide the earliest commencement date of their registers. The information is tabulated in alphabetical order by civil parish name within each of Ireland's thirty-two counties. To assist in identifying the location of each civil parish the appropriate map reference number was recorded to *A New Genealogical Atlas of Ireland* (By Brian Mitchell, Genealogical Publishing Company, Baltimore, 1986) and to the maps accompanying the Householders' Index (compiled by the National Library of Ireland, Dublin) to the Griffith's Valuation.

In A *Guide to Irish Churches and Graveyards* (by Brian Mitchell, Genealogical Publishing Company, Baltimore, 1990) every church and graveyard in Ireland at the time of the mid-19th century Griffith's Valuation was identified in relation to a townland or street address. Each townland or street (in a town) was located within its appropriate civil parish, and each civil parish was listed in alphabetical order within its county. An Ordnance Survey number was provided to enable the researcher to pinpoint the exact location of any church or graveyard on a six-inch Ordnance Survey map.

As the major denominations produce directories annually it is relatively straightforward to identify the contact name and address of the present-day incumbents of churches in Ireland. The *Irish Catholic Directory* identifies, within dioceses, details of Roman Catholic parishes and the priests serving them. The *Church of Ireland Directory* lists its parishes and ministers on a diocesan basis, and the Presbyterian Church records the appropriate detail by congregation, within Presbyteries, in the *Presbyterian Church in Ireland Directory*.

If you intend to visit a minister of a church, in person, I would recommend that you make contact in advance either by writing or by telephone. If you turn up unannounced at their door step there is no guarantee that you will receive the welcome you would like. I must admit I would prefer searching through a copy of a church register, at my leisure, as opposed to a hurried examination of a register in the presence of an impatient clergyman.

You should also attempt to find out something about the history of the church associated with your ancestor. The number of books detailing the histories of churches, either individually or collectively, is growing by the year. *A History of Congregations in the Presbyterian Church in Ireland, 1610-1982* (the Presbyterian Historical Society of Ireland, Belfast, 1982), for example, gives a brief history of every Presbyterian congregation in Ireland.

Using County Londonderry as an example there are a number of very useful reference works on church history. In 1999 The Ulster Historical Foundation, Belfast published *Clergy of Derry and Raphoe* which brings right up to date Canon Leslie's monumental achievement of detailing the history of each Church of Ireland parish in the diocese of Derry and Raphoe (which extends over Counties Derry, Donegal and Tyrone). In addition he provided biographical detail on the clergy in these parishes, including many from pre-Reformation times.

*An Introduction to the Parishes of Derry Diocese* produced by Thomas Bradley and Finbar Madden (published 2000) records short histories of all Roman Catholic parishes within the Diocese of Derry. Books such as these are useful in attempting to find out when an original parish was subdivided to establish a new parish. For example the book records that the parish of Greencastle, County Tyrone was originally part of Lower Badoney but in 1892 it became a separate parish.

Histories of 30 Presbyterian congregations in Counties Derry and Antrim are recorded in Julia Mullin's book *The Presbytery of Coleraine* (published 1979). Julia Mullin also compiled histories of a further 12 congregations in County Derry in her book *The Presbytery of Limavady* (published by North-West Books, Limavady, 1989).

Having decided on a register to search, you will have to resist the impulse to glance quickly through the pages, stopping only briefly at those surnames which you think might belong to your ancestors. The registers, especially of a later date, may be tabulated and the information written in the appropriate columns, neatly and legibly. But often the information is simply written, and not too clearly at that, in sentence form. The implications for the impatient will be to overlook the very entry you are looking for. Surnames can be difficult to interpret and distinguish in the context of a poor quality, handwritten parish register.

It must also be remembered (see chapter on *The Importance of Surnames in Family History*) that standardisation in the spelling of surnames is a 20th century phenomenon. You should always be aware of possible variants of your family name. There may even be instances where potential variant spellings of a surname cannot be predicted. It is also possible that the original compiler of a record made a mistake. With care and patience, however, you will lessen the chances of misreading a surname, and increase the likelihood of interpreting not very legible handwriting.

# Church Registers

An invaluable source for family historians for the period prior to civil registration. This source should always be checked if you know the civil parish address and religious denomination of your ancestor:

A **baptism entry** can provide the name of the child; date and location of baptism; date of birth; parents' names including maiden name of mother; parents' address (by townland); occupation; and names of sponsors (particularly in the Roman Catholic registers).

A **marriage entry** can provide the names of the bride and groom; their places of residence; date and location of marriage; parents' names (including occasionally the maiden name of the mother); and names of witnesses.

**Burial records** can provide the name and residence of the deceased; burial date and place; occasionally the age of the deceased. In the case of children, the names of parents may be included.

## BENEFITS

1. Before civil registration they offer, in many cases, the only means to identify a birth, marriage or death of an ancestor.
2. They provide sufficient information to confirm the nature of relationships between named individuals.
3. If a townland address is recorded they make searches of other sources such as census records, Tithe Books and Griffith's Valuation very straightforward.
4. Copies of most church registers are held in record offices such as the National Library, Dublin and the Public Record Office, Belfast.

## LIMITATIONS

1. Access to this source is through knowledge of the parish address of your ancestor. Many people tracing their Irish roots know at best the county of origin of their ancestor.
2. This source (unless you commission a search of the databases of the genealogy centres in Ireland ) is not indexed, so searching a register can be very time consuming.
3. Owing to the seemingly complex ecclesiastical structure in Ireland of parishes and congregations; to the destruction of many Church of Ireland registers; and to the late commencement of many Roman Catholic and Presbyterian registers, it isn't always straightforward to identify the appropriate registers to search.
4. Dates of commencement and amount of information vary. The oldest registers tend to be those of the Church of Ireland, and in many early registers (of all denominations) townland names and, in marriage registers, the names of parents are not provided.
5. Poor handwriting, poor condition and non-tabulated layout of many registers makes transcription difficult. Patience is the keyword when searching church registers.
6. There is no standardisation in either the spelling of townland names or surnames in church registers. Always be aware of possible variants of your family name and of your ancestor's townland address.

The patience and care taken in searching church registers is well worth the effort. If you are very fortunate you might be able to follow successive generations through the registers of one church. A summary of the benefits and limitations of church registers can be seen on the enclosed table (see page 61).

The value of church registers as a source is now demonstrated with a search through the registers of Shankill Parish Church, Church of Ireland, Lurgan, County Armagh for references to the Corner/Cordner branch of my family tree.

My starting point into the Corner/Cordner branch of the family tree was the identification of the following civil marriage certificate: George John Wake, a merchant of Lurgan married Catherine Cordner of Toberhewny in Shankill Parish Church, Church of Ireland, Lurgan on 6 May 1874. Catherine's father was recorded as Henry Cordner, a farmer.

The Townland Index confirms that the townland of Toberhewny is located in the civil parish of Shankill, County Armagh. As it was customary to marry in the bride's parish it meant that the obvious church register to search for additional Cordner details was that of Shankill Church of Ireland Church. A microfilm copy of the registers of Shankill Parish Church (MIC1/18) was searched in the Public Record Office, Belfast. The following details were recorded:

**Baptism Register**

| | |
|---|---|
| 5 March 1845 | Henry of parents Henry and Letitia Corner of Toberhuney |
| 5 May 1849 | Thomas of parents Henry and Letitia Corner of Toberhuney |
| 28 December 1853 | Jane of parents Henry and Letitia Corner of Toberhuney |
| 26 March 1856 | George of parents Henry and Letitia Corner of Toberhuney |
| 24 November 1859 | William John of parents Henry and Letitia Corner of Toberhuney |

**Marriage Register**

| | |
|---|---|
| 23 April 1844 | Henry Corner of Toberhuney in this parish, bachelor and Letitia Mathews of Cornreaney in the parish of Donaghcloney, Spinster. By license |

**Baptism Register**

| | |
|---|---|
| 11 July 1824 | Henry of parents Henry and May Corner of Lurgan |

**Marriage Register**

Unsuccessful search for marriage of Henry Corner to May.

Four Corner marriages in the period 1802 to 1824 were identified:

| | |
|---|---|
| 23 August 1813 | Thomas Corner to Margaret Douglas |
| 21 December 1815 | Thomas Corner to Mary Summerton |
| 31 July 1817 | John Corner to Mary Barrit |
| 21 April 1822 | Robert Corner to Isabella Hynd |

Until additional information comes to light I will not be able to prove the relevance or otherwise of any of the above four marriage entries.

The next logical step in searching the above family history would be to extend the search for the marriage of Henry Corner to May to the registers of other Protestant churches in the civil parish of Shankill. The town of Lurgan is located in the civil parish of Shankill. Unfortunately the registers of the Methodist Church and Presbyterian churches in Lurgan don't exist for the period 1800 to 1824. The marriage registers, on the other hand, of the Religious Society of Friends (ie Quakers) in Lurgan commence in 1632. Thus it is quite possible that an unsuccessful search for the marriage of Henry Corner to May, at this stage, may simply mean that the marriage occurred before the keeping of church registers.

A decision could also be made to extend the search for the above marriage to the Protestant churches in the parishes surrounding Shankill parish. There is no doubt that the vast majority of marriages were between people who lived locally. The above family history confirms this: George Wake of Lurgan married Catherine Cordner of Toberhewny. This townland lies on the southern boundary of the town of Lurgan. Henry Corner of Toberhewny married Letitia Mathews of Cornreany. Although these two townlands are in different counties (ie Armagh and Down respectively) the Corner and Mathews farms shared a common boundary! It might be worthwhile, therefore, to search the registers of the Protestant churches in the civil parish of Donaghcloney (ie the civil parish in which the townland of Cornreany is located). The Church of Ireland registers for Donaghcloney Parish Church commence in 1697.

Although church registers are perhaps the single most valuable source in genealogy it doesn't mean that your research is finished once you have exhausted them. You should always look on any information you gain from one source as offering clues to other records to search. Always remember that no record source, no matter how important, stands in isolation.

The above family detail recorded in church baptismal and marriage registers should provide encouragement to begin searches of other sources for additional information. For example the civil death registers recorded the deaths of Henry Cordner and Letitia Cordner on 25 August 1887 and 18 September 1889 respectively. The will of Henry Cordner of Toberhewny which was proved at the Armagh Probate Office on 5 November 1891 named many family members.

The Tithe Book of 1833 records a Henry Corner with 2 farms of land amounting to 6 acres at Toberhewny. By the time of the Griffith's Valuation in 1864 Henry Cordner was farming 6 acres in Toberhewny and a William Cordner was farming 10 acres.

The Griffith's Valuation confirms that Lord Lurgan was the landlord of the townland of Toberhewny. Toberhewny is part of the manor of Brownlowsderry owned by the Brownlows, Lords Lurgan. The records of that key Irish institution, the great landed estate, are a vast source of untapped knowledge.

Estate and personal papers of the Brownlow family, Lords Lurgan relating largely to the manors of Brownlowsderry and Richmount in the Lurgan area, County Armagh are deposited in the Public Record Office, Belfast. Some 500 volumes and 5000 documents relating to the Brownlow estate can be found in the Public Record Office of Northern Ireland (Reference D1928).

A map contained in a survey of the estate of Charles Brownlow by Alex Richmond in 1832 (T2485/2/4, PRONI) identifies 2 small farms of 5 and 6 acres being farmed by H Corner. No Corners or Cordners, however, were recorded in Toberhuney at the time of Patrick Dougan's survey of the estate of William Brownlow in 1751 (T2485/2/1). The 1766 religious census for the parish of Shankill did record a William Corner in Tuberhuney.

The Brownlow Leasebook of 1667-1711 was published by the Public Record Office of Northern Ireland in 1988 as *Settlement and Survival on an Ulster Estate* (edited by R G Gillespie). This leasebook was drawn up by Arthur Brownlow, the estate's owner between 1667 and 1711. This leasebook records that the tenants of Toberhewny in 1667 were Robert Gare, Anthonie Hartlowe, William Jones, Jane Porter and William Smith. The leasebook recorded two Corner leases, one in the townland of Drumnamoe in the civil parish of Shankill and the other in the townland of Derryadd in Montiaghs civl parish, County Armagh:

*Parryes land 21 acre and Levyes land 15 acre in Dromenmoe leased to Henry Corner for his life at £6 3s per annum above taxes; rest as usual dated 15 August 1695.*

*Derriadde to Edward Murphy, John Abraham and William Corner for 21 years from May 1691...dated 3rd November 1690*

The leasebook also recorded a copy of Arthur Brownlow's will dated 29 September 1710 with one of the witnesses being H Corner.

In short an examination of church registers is well worth the effort. Finally, of major significance to family historians, especially to those who don't know the civil parish address of their ancestor, is the computerisation of church registers by the network of local centres in the Irish Genealogical Project (see chapter on *Genealogy Centres in Ireland - How to make the best use of them).*

## Genealogy Centres in Ireland
### How to make the best use of them

Some 50 million North Americans and 5 million Australians claim to have Irish ancestry. It is estimated that in the US alone 35 million people have an interest in genealogy. Genealogy is the third most popular hobby in the United States and the second most popular topic on the Internet. In a recent study of subscribers to AT & T's Internet access service, it was found that 31% had gone online primarily to search for ancestors. It is not surprising, therefore, that the Tourist Boards in Ireland see genealogy and tracing ones ancestors as a potential marketing opportunity. I think it is fair to say that there is still uncertainty on how best to develop this market.

The Irish Genealogical Project (IGP) became a reality in 1990. The IGP envisaged the establishment of a network of centres, usually on a county basis, to computerise the major record sources and to service family history queries within their catchment areas. The following sources have been identified as the major sources to be computerised:
- Pre-1922 civil birth, marriage and death registers
- Pre-1900 church baptismal, marriage and burial registers of **all** denominations
- Gravestone Inscriptions
- 1901 census
- Mid-19th century Griffith's Valuation
- Early-19th century Tithe Applotment Books

This network of centres and their associated databases became, in the 1990s, the linchpin of "ancestral heritage" promotions of Bord Failte and The Northern Ireland Tourist Board. Without public funding through government-funded training programmes the creation of databases of this scale and complexity would not have been feasible.

The scale of this achievement can be gauged by an examination of the enclosed table of sources computerised by one centre since 1990. The Derry Genealogy Centre database which is dedicated to County Derry and the Inishowen Peninsula, County Donegal now stands at some 1 million records.

Full details of all the IGP genealogy centres can be found on the Irish Family History Foundation's site on the Internet at www.irishroots.net. The Foundation's home page also provides some useful general advice. For example under the heading MAKING A START it offers the following advice:

*In order to make an initial search of any of the research centres' databases possible a certain amount of starting information is required:*

- *The name of one's Irish-born emigrant ancestor*
- *The emigrant's father's name*
- *the mother's pre-marriage surname*
- *an approximate year of birth*

# DERRY GENEALOGY CENTRE

## RECORDS INDEXED

### 1) Roman Catholic Parish Registers (pre-1900) - 200,000 entries

County Donegal - Buncrana, Carndonagh, Clonmany, Culdaff, Doneyloop, Fahan, Iskaheen, Killygordon, Lifford, Malin, Moville and St Johnston.

County Derry - Bellaghy, Claudy, Coleraine, Desertmartin, Draperstown, Dungiven, Faughanvale, Feeny, Garvagh, Greenlough, Kilrea, Lavey, Limavady, Maghera and Magilligan; and Long Tower, St Eugene's and Waterside in Derry City.

### 2) Church of Ireland Registers (pre-1864) - 50,000 entries

County Derry - Agherton, Ballinderry, Castlerock, Christ Church (Derry), Desertlyn, Desertmartin, Draperstown, Drumachose, Dunboe, Dungiven, Fermoyle, Glendermott, Kilrea, St Columb's Cathedral, Tamlaghtard and Tamlaght Finlagan.

### 3) Presbyterian Registers (pre-1864) - 50,000 entries

County Derry - Balteagh, Ballywatt, Boveedy, Bovevagh, Castledawson, Castlerock, First Coleraine, Coleraine - New Row, Derramore, Drumachose, Second Dunboe, Dungiven, Faughanvale, First Garvagh, Gortnessy, Second Kilrea, Largy, Maghera, First Magherafelt, Moneydig, First and Second Moneymore, Portrush, Portstewart, Scriggan and Swatragh; and Ballyarnett, First Derry, Carlisle Road (Fourth Derry) and Strand (Second Derry) in Derry City.

### 4) Civil Marriage Registers for County Derry - 75,000 entries
|  |  |
|---|---|
| All Protestant Churches | 1845-1921 |
| All Roman Catholic Churches | 1864-1921 |

### 5) Civil Birth Registers for County Derry (1864-1921) - 200,000 entries

Derry City and Ballykelly, Bellarena, Claudy, Coleraine, Draperstown (to 1897), Dungiven, Eglinton, Feeny, Limavady, Magherafelt and Moneymore .

### 6) Census Substitutes for County Derry (these list heads of household only)
|  |  |
|---|---|
| 1663 Hearth Money Rolls | ) |
| 1740 Protestant Householders Lists | ) |
| 1766 Religious Census Returns | )    25,451 entries |
| 1796 Flax Growers Lists | ) |

Early-19th century Tithe Books - 41,606 entries
1831 Census - 40,769 entries
Mid-19th century Griffith's Valuation - 56,374 entries

### 7) The 1901 Census for County Derry and Inishowen Peninsula, County Donegal - 187,000 entries

### 8) Gravestone Inscriptions for 110 graveyards in County Derry - 65,000 entries.

### 9) Passenger Lists through the port of Derry for the years 1803-1806, 1833-1835 and 1847-1871

A number of Ireland's genealogy centres have developed their own sites on the Internet. For example the Ulster Historical Foundation in Belfast have set up a very informative and well designed site at www.ancestryireland.com.

On their Ancestral Research Service page the Ulster Historical Foundation state: *The success of the search is partly determined by the quality of information supplied. Those wishing to commission research should provide as much information as possible about the place of origin of ancestors in Ireland (eg county, parish or, preferably, townland) and their religion (eg Roman Catholic, Church of Ireland or Presbyterian). The quality of initial information supplied will determine the success of the search.*

The potential of the Internet is virtually unlimited. For example, for those people whose roots lie in County Kilkenny your first visit should be to County Kilkenny Ireland Genealogy and History at www.rootsweb.com/~irlkik. This site provides access to maps and information on history, placenames and sources.

The magazine *Irish Roots* produces annually, in its summer issue, a **Directory of Irish Genealogical Resources** which includes an updated list of all of Ireland's genealogy research centres. This update provides the contact details of each centre together with their opening times, sources searched, cost of research and length of time required to compile reports.

The benefits of the databases created by the network of centres under the auspices of the Irish Genealogical project (IGP) are not in doubt.

Databases speed up research significantly and, therefore, they should reduce the cost of a genealogical search to the client. Traditionally genealogical research has been charged by the hour. It is the time spent identifying and searching through record sources, as opposed to a payment for expertise, which makes up the bulk of fees charged by professional genealogists.

Databases, furthermore, increase flexibility as records can be indexed and, therefore, searched under any field name. For example civil birth records are currently indexed by name of child - once computerised family group searches become very feasible as searches can be conducted using the parents' names.

One example will sum up the value of databases to genealogy. It took the staff of the Derry Genealogy Centre 3 years to input and validate the pre-1900 baptism, marriage and burial registers of all Roman Catholic parishes in Counties Derry and Donegal which are located in the Diocese of Derry. This database of 30 parishes can now be searched for any entry and by any combination of field names in a matter of seconds.

Guidelines were drawn up by the IGP to ensure the creation of accurate databases. Many records of value to the family historian are handwritten, and suffering from wear and tear. A database is only as good as the information it contains. If information is not entered or it is not entered correctly it effectively means that details about your ancestor have been lost.

It must also be pointed out that there is nothing a database can do to rectify a situation where data doesn't exist in the first place. The absence of relevant records is a well known problem in Irish genealogy as many records were destroyed or simply not recorded until quite late on.

In *Irish Roots* (issue 1994 Number 4) the question was put: who can tie into pre-1600 Irish lineages? The answer given was *"probably only descendants of those families who remained prominent through the early 1800s can hope for such a connection. The fact is that the lineages of Catholic peasant emigrants from Ireland often can only be traced back to about 1800, because Catholic records are largely lacking prior to the nineteenth century"*.

It must also be emphasised that there will always be errors in databases. In an article in USA TODAY (Wednesday, 18 November 1998) Rick Hampson reported on the efforts of Mormon volunteers to index the records of the 17 million immigrants who came through New York Harbour from 1892 to 1924. His article was titled *Smudges, scribbles hold Ellis Island's history* with the subtitle *Database is painstaking - and painful - work*. One expert estimated that at least 10% of the names will be irretrievable, ie about 1.7 million immigrants. Several reasons were given for why some people will not find their ancestors' names:

- Spellings and even entire names change over the years. The name a descendant searches for may not be the one an ancestor entered the country under.
- Some names or other information will be misread and incorrectly entered into the database.
- Some people simply didn't immigrate through New York, even though they or their descendants think they did.
- Some names are illegible and can't be included in the database.

All the above reasons are equally valid in the context of a parish register entered in an IGP database. The IGP databases, by recording all variant spellings and attaching them to a standard spelling of the surname, have attempted to deal with that Irish phenomenon of surname variants. In the Derry Genealogy Centre database there are 83 variants of the surname Doherty, including Daugherty, Docherty, O'Dogherty and many others. Other examples of variant spellings of the same surname in the Derry database include:

- Mulhern, Mackilherin, McIlherron and McElhern
- McHugh, McCue, McHue and McKew
- Cumins, Cummins, McCummins and Miskimmons
- Small, Smalley and Kilky

It is very easy to make errors in transcription. In terms of tracing your family history an error, for example, which changes an ancestor's surname will have disastrous consequences. Such errors, in effect, mean that you have lost somebody's ancestor. A few examples of totally different surnames which can be difficult to interpret and distinguish in the context of a poor quality, handwritten parish register include:

- Greer, Green and Greeve
- Irvine and Irwin

- Ryan and Regan
- Barratt and Barnett
- Semple and Temple
- Carter and Carten
- Millen and Miller

In addition to interpretation problems in handwritten records it can also be frustrating when the record compiler leaves out some additional information. I still remember the burial entry recorded by one parish priest which in the context of tracing ancestry one century later was of little value. The burial entry simply read "Big Ned's Sister".

It is also quite possible that the original compiler of a record made a mistake. For example in one case we worked on the child was baptised as Robert John King but recorded as Samuel King in his birth certificate.

In undertaking research for clients through the Derry Genealogy Centre database we noticed on a significant number of occasions that we could identify a post-1864 Roman Catholic marriage in church registers but not in the civil marriage records. In theory all Roman Catholic marriages were subject to civil registration from 1864.

On one occasion I selected 20 marriages recorded in 1871 from one Roman Catholic church register and attempted to locate them in the civil marriage registers. As far as I could tell only 7 of them had been registered in the civil marriage registers. From a genealogical point of view this is disappointing as civil marriage registers usually record more information than Roman Catholic Church marriage registers. For example civil marriage registers record the names of the fathers of bride and groom but the actual entries in the registers kept by the Roman Catholic parishes usually don't.

As genealogy centres have built up databases for their local areas that can't be matched by any other organisation there is no doubting the value of these centres to the family historian. If you lack the time or interest to pursue your family history it makes very good sense to commission a centre to search their database and compile a report into your family history. As Oscar Wilde said "a genealogist is a person who will trace your ancestors as far back as your money will go". Genealogy centres, in compiling a research report, will charge no more or no less than many professional genealogists.

Genealogy Centres, furthermore, should have the added advantage of local knowledge of the area you are interested in. They may be able to identify place names and the locations of old graveyards; they may know of useful local publications and record sources; and they will have some knowledge of the general history of the area.

Some preparatory work into the area of interest to a family historian should give some clues as to the value of commissioning research. For example if you are researching an ancestor who lived in the parish of Faughanvale, County

Londonderry it is highly unlikely that you will find any relevant birth or marriage entries prior to 1802. The reason for this is quite simply that no church registers of any denomination predate 1802.

There are, of course, a number of reference works, arranged by county and/or record sources, which you can consult yourself to identify relevant record sources for a particular area. Examples include *Irish Genealogy A Record Finder* (edited by Donal Begley, Heraldic Artists, Dublin, 1981), *Irish Records - Sources For Family and Local History* (James Ryan, Ancestry Publishing, Utah, 1988), *A Guide to Irish Parish Registers* (Brian Mitchell, Genealogical Publishing Company, Baltimore, 1988) and *A Guide to Irish Churches and Graveyards* (edited by Brian Mitchell, Genealogical Publishing Company, Baltimore, 1990).

I think it is fair to say that if you have already exhausted the major sources of genealogical research in Ireland, ie church registers, civil registers, census returns and census substitutes, there is probably little additional information to be gained from commissioning a genealogy centre to search their database. In these circumstances you might wish to consider employing a professional genealogist to examine more specialist sources which may, or may not, produce results. There are no shortcuts in family history. All potential sources should be searched. It also goes without saying that if you expect someone else to carry out the necessary research you will have to pay for their time.

I would also recommend that if you don't know at least the county of origin of your ancestor you should not commission either a professional genealogist or genealogy centre to conduct research.

There is no doubt that the IGP databases increase the likelihood of identifying your ancestor. In the age before computers a fairly precise knowledge (usually a townland or parish address) of where an ancestor came from was the key to unlocking family history. As most records of genealogical value were compiled by civil parish it meant that effective genealogical research in Ireland required knowledge of the civil parish in which your ancestor lived. As a general rule the knowledge of the county of origin of your ancestor was insufficient evidence for locating them.

The starting point, however, for many Americans seeking their Irish ancestry is at best the knowledge of the county of origin of their family. In these circumstances the database of a genealogy centre is essential to assist such people identify their ancestral origins. It will be for many the only realistic hope to locate the ancestral home.

Access to church registers, in the absence of indexes, is gained through knowledge of the parish address and religious denomination of your ancestor. If, for example, all you know about your ancestor is that he was Presbyterian and came from County Londonderry this effectively means that details of your ancestor could be contained in any one of the registers of the 68 Presbyterian congregations located in this county. It is quite feasible, however, for a computer to search all 68 registers (provided they have been inputted) for the required details.

If you want to conduct your own family history research then genealogy centres, the way they are currently organised, are probably not going to satisfy you. Owing to contractual agreements with church authorities they can't give the public direct access to the database. Furthermore, as many genealogy centres have to raise extra funds to survive it is only natural that they will charge people who require their databases to be searched. I would still, however, contact the centre of interest to you as they may be willing to share their knowledge of the local area. I think it is fair to say that if you write or email such requests you will probably only receive back a standard reply requesting you to fill in a research form. If, however, you are in Ireland and doing some local research you have nothing to lose by visiting the local centre and making enquiries. I have had many visitors to the Derry Genealogy Centre who have received free advice!

I believe there is one circumstance in which genealogy centres offer real value for money. If all you know about your ancestor is their county of origin then the database of the appropriate genealogy centre is probably the only realistic hope of confirming your ancestral origins. Without the help of such a database you hold insufficient information to make basic decisions about which sources to search.

I think most observers are impressed with the scale and all-Ireland dimension of the IGP databases. Criticism is largely confined to how this information is made available.

The Irish Ancestral Research Association (TIARA) invited its members in 1997 to comment on the research services offered by the network of genealogy centres in Ireland. Survey participants were asked to give a ranking of Unacceptable, Acceptable or Exceptional. The report can be viewed on the Internet at http://world.std.com/~ahern/results.htm. Some of the comments included:
- The quality and quantity of information between centres varies
- Need to regulate fees charged and set standards for each genealogy centre. "There is a great deal of confusion and variation in the fees charged by the individual centres ... It suggest poor central control".
- There should be a provision for a single record search fee
- The databases should be made available to the public to search. "It is of minimal help to have a stranger searching based on information he obtained from an overly restrictive form."
- All centres should have email
- Offer online searches via the Internet

In an ideal world the information on the IGP databases could be accessed from anywhere in the world for either no fee or a small fee. *Irish Roots* (Issue 1995 Number 1), for example, voiced the opinion that the IGP has the technology to combine all the local databases into one large, 32 county database and make it accessible by E-mail to homes all over the world. At present local centres receive sustainable funding (and, therefore, survival) on the basis of their ability to meet the demands of government training programmes, not on their ability to satisfy visitors. A central, coordinating body, with very specific tourism aims and with limited funds, will always have difficulty forging a common purpose among 35 centres,

71

who are largely funded locally through training schemes and any revenue they can generate.

A comprehensive review of the Irish Genealogical Project was published in December 1996 by the Department of the Taoiseach. It concluded that the IGP still had "the potential to produce significant economic, social, cultural and political benefits to Ireland". The Irish Government continues to feel that there exists a "compelling case for supporting and resourcing the central management of IGP". This was despite the fact that they had some harsh things to say about the accuracy of the IGP database. It suggested up to 10% of the records have "critical errors". In a debate in the Dail it was reported that the IGP had developed in an "ad hoc and honky tonk way" and that there had been a lack of effective management and co-ordination. It was also suggested that in the age of the Internet the project needed to be re-evaluated.

At present it does seem that genealogy centres in Ireland are moving towards offering a high price, high quality, value-added service. There is a growing perception that if you want an in-depth, well presented, attractively bound and costly report then genealogy centres want to hear from you. On the other hand if all you want is a quick, cheap search for a name in a particular source the welcome is perhaps not quite so warm. From a business point of view there is nothing wrong with this approach if it generates the revenue you require.

I am not convinced, however, that this is the correct approach from a tourism point of view. Evidence would seem to suggest that the majority of people interested in genealogy want to do their own research. I felt that a great strength of the Derry Genealogy Centre was its ability to offer quick, relatively cheap searches of an unrivalled, localised computer database.

I still remember a European Heritage Consultant telling his audience at a Conference on Developing Heritage Attractions held in Dublin in October 1990 that 95% of museums are geared towards the "scholarly" visitor yet they only make up 5% of visitors. He stated that 20% of visitors to museums can be termed as "interested" and 75% as "casual". If this sort of breakdown also applies to genealogy centres it is possible that in appealing to the 5% of family historians who want high price, comprehensive research reports, genealogy centres are failing to meet the requirements of the other 95% who would like their help or advice at either no cost or at a more realistic price level.

The Tourist Boards, both North and South, see family history as a means to draw increasing numbers of long-staying, high-spending, overseas visitors to Ireland. The money generated at research centres is insignificant compared to the indirect spin-offs to the economy from visitors seeking their roots (ie by taking a holiday in Ireland). In 1996 the Northern Ireland Tourist Board estimated that 72,000 US visitors (ie 5% of visitors) spent £20.1 million (ie 10% of tourist revenue). In 1996 US Visitors (with 80% from either California or the East Coast) spent on average £279 and stayed 8 nights. In the same year 28,000 Canadians (with 60% from the Province of Ontario) visited Northern Ireland, spending on average £321 and staying 10 nights.

I believe that the databases and local knowledge built up by the genealogy centres should be integrated into the already existing network of public funded, tourist information centres. This would ultimately result in more satisfied customers and, it would encourage more people to visit Ireland and the homeland of their ancestors. During the off-peak season genealogy centres could be busy answering queries and/or conducting research for those intending to visit the ancestral homeland the following Spring or Summer. Genealogy centres would thus become part of the tourism network contributing to a quality holiday experience in Ireland. Any money generated from research activities could then contribute towards at least some of the running costs of operating a research service.

Donn Devine, an American professional genealogist in a letter to *Irish Roots* (Issue 1994 Number 1) claimed: *Many who have not already visited Ireland will do so as soon as they identify the locality where their forbears lived....Centres that furnish extractions to overseas clients can expect most will eventually visit as tourists....For the DIY researcher who knows what he or she wants, Heritage Centres should be able to furnish it promptly on an advertised per-name-extracted basis, without repeated exchanges of letters, registration, deposits, and all-or-nothing research packages.*

To conclude, the network of genealogy centres might not be organised the way you would like them to be, but their databases are a fantastic achievement. These databases were built by unemployed young people under the supervision of dedicated, and not particularly well-paid, supervisors. And as we all know in this changing world these databases could be accessed, via the Internet, on your mobile phone - if that is the way the Irish Genealogical Project wishes to proceed.

As manager of the Derry Genealogy Centre I always told visitors that there was no way that our database could compete with the Mormon's International Genealogical Index (IGI) on a world scale. But equally there was no way that the IGI could compete with the Derry database at the local level. I always had supreme confidence in the quality of our database, I never felt the need for a "hard sell". If a visitor couldn't see the benefits of the database I never tried to change their opinion. As far as I was concerned the database did the talking.

# Local History and the Family Historian

It would seem to me that in the US and Canada popular historical research is centred on genealogical research while in Ireland it is very much focused on local history. This doesn't mean that people in Ireland are not interested in family history. Indeed the sources used by the family historian and the local historian are essentially the one and the same. Local history, however, tends to concentrate on the community that has lived in a townland, village, parish or even town.

In *Pathways to Ulster's Past - Sources and Resources for Local Studies* Peter Collins (The Institute of Irish Studies, Belfast, 1998) states that Local History is one of the fastest-growing interests in Ireland today. The book details sources such as:

- state papers, surveys, yeomanry lists, poll tax returns
- hearth money rolls, censuses, valuation records
- ordnance survey, education records, magistrate reports
- parliamentary commissions, land records, legal records
- wills, church records, gravestone inscriptions, maps
- directories, newspapers, journals and photographs

These sources are very familiar to family historians. Peter Collins defines local history as follows: "Usually local history refers to a specifically defined, delineated and discrete area, with the emphasis on the community in that area. Any source or resource that tells us about a particular locality constitutes the raw material of local history."

The study of local history has a fine pedigree in Ireland. One of the most significant local history projects ever conducted in Ireland was carried out by the Ordnance Survey in the 1830s. In 1824, as a prelude to a nationwide valuation of land and buildings, ie the Griffith's Valuation, the Ordnance Survey was directed to map Ireland at a scale of 6 inches to one mile. The survey was directed by Colonel Thomas Colby, who had available to him officers of the Royal Engineers and three companies of sappers and miners. The resultant 6 inch maps, in effect a record of Ireland's 60,462 townlands, were published between 1835 and 1846.

It was intended to accompany each map with written topographical descriptions for every civil parish. Only one, namely the Parish of Templemore, County Londonderry was published prior to the Government discontinuing the Survey on the grounds of expense in 1840. The field officers did, however, gather much historical, geographical, economic and social information for many parishes, especially for the northern half of Ireland. These manuscripts, which were deposited in 52 boxes in the Royal Irish Academy, Dublin, provide a unique insight into life in Ireland in the 1830s.

**The framework of the memoirs was as follows:**

Section I        Geography or Natural State

1.      Name
2.      Locality (ie position, size, boundaries)
3.      Natural state:
        a) natural features: hills; lakes; rivers; bogs; woods; coast; climate
        b) natural history: botany; zoology; geology

Section II       Topography or artificial state.

1.      Modern: towns; public buildings; gentleman's seats; bleach greens, manufacturers, mills, etc; communications
2.      Ancient (ecclesiastical buildings; military buildings; remains of pagan or unknown origin)
3.      General appearance and scenery

Section III      The people, or present state

1.      Social economy: early improvements; obstructions to improvements; local government; dispensaries; schools; poor; religion; habits of the people; emigration; remarkable events
2.      Productive economy:
        a) manufacturing or commercial; fairs and markets
        b) rural: grazing; cattle; uses made of bogs; drainage; planting; fishing

Section IV

1.      Divisions (other than counties, baronies, parishes, and townlands)
2.      Townlands

A team based at the Institute of Irish Studies, Queen's University of Belfast has now transcribed, indexed and published the complete set of the Ordnance Survey Memoirs in 40 volumes. By examining the Institute's web site at www.qub.qc.uk/iis/publications/OrdnanceSurveyMemoirs it is quite straightforward to identify the volume which will give much insight into the parish your ancestor lived in. These 40 volumes "act as a nineteenth-century Domesday book and are essential to the understanding of the cultural heritage of our communities."

The Memoirs can provide much useful genealogical information (for the 1830s) as in many instances emigrants, farmers and mill owners were named:

**Kilmore Parish, County Armagh**
**Rockmacreeny Townland**: proprietor Mr Bacon, agent C Brush Esq... Farms from 6 to 64 acres, the largest is occupied by R Williamson. Rent from 22s to 25s 6d, soil good and in a high state of cultivation. It contains a flax mill and 2 old forts. Market Tanderagee, 5 miles distant.

**Loughgilly Parish, County Armagh**

**Mills in Drumharif**: Corn mill, in the townland of Drumharif, belongs to Dennis Boyle, diameter of wheel 12 feet, breadth 1 foot 6 inches, fall of water 4 feet, breast wheel. (In the 1830s most corn and flax mills were powered by water wheels.)

**Clonmany Parish, County Donegal**

**River Fishing**: the right of fishing belongs to the Revd W H Harvey and he has let it for 5 years to Mr Halliday of Derry, from Binnion to Ned's battery in Lough Swilly, for 30 pounds a year.

**Clonmany Parish, County Donegal**

**Proprietors**: The principal proprietors under Lord Donegall, who is the chief landlord, are the Revd W H Harvey, whose lands are at present held by Mrs Merrick, viz. Urismana, Leenan, Dunaff, Letter, Kenaght, Tallagh, Cleagh and Altahalla. The Dogherty family possess Straid, Anney, Ardagh, Lonebratly, Ballymacmurty and part of Ruskey. Mr Loghery possesses Dunally; Archdeacon Torrens holds Magherymore; Miss Harvey, Cloontagh; Sir A Chichester and the Revd S Montgomery, each a part of Ballyliffin; Mr Curry, Straas and Rashanny; Councillor Dobbs, Carrareagh; Mr Cary, Fugart; Mr Harvey of Malin Hall, Legacury and Carrickabracky and part of Ruskey; Ardervil, Mindoran and Gaddyduff belong to the church.

The Ordnance Survey memoirs for Counties Antrim and Londonderry are unique in that for many of their parishes lists of emigrants for a few years in the mid- to late-1830s were compiled. As emigration records these lists are unparalleled. They identify both the destinations of the emigrants and their places of origin in Ireland. For example the memoir for Glynn Parish, County Antrim records that in 1839 the Blair family from the townland of Ballyvernstown, William, age 31, Jane, 30 and their children William John, 7, Sarah, 4 and Mary, 2 emigrated to St John, New Brunswick, Canada. The emigrant lists from the Ordnance Survey memoirs of Counties Antrim and Londonderry were published in *Irish Emigration Lists 1833-1839* (edited by Brian Mitchell, Genealogical Publishing Company, Baltimore, 1989).

The study of local history is now seen as an integral part of education in our schools in Ireland. Dr Brian K Lambkin, Director, Centre for Migration Studies at the Ulster American Folk Park, Omagh (details on Internet at www.folkpark.com) has proposed a *Connecting Our Place in Time* Project to support the introduction of Citizenship education in Northern Ireland. Its focus is on learning about citizenship through learning about the local community. Its main aim is to enable the individual pupil to develop a sense of belonging to their local community and a sense of where and how they fit into the larger scheme of things. *Connecting Our Place in Time* aims to promote the study by primary and secondary schools of their local area, how they have developed, and how they are connected to networks of various kinds (political, economic, social, cultural) at regional, national and international levels. In this context Place is seen to operate at 4 levels, the local, the regional, the national and the international.

This *Connecting Our Place* project builds on a remarkable growth in local studies in recent years in Ireland especially at the level of the smallest unit of civil administration, the townland. It is argued this "demonstrates the importance of studying units with which people had a strong sense of identification".

In *Townlands in Ulster: Local History Studies* (ed W H Crawford and R H Foy, Ulster Historical Foundation, Belfast, 1998) an attempt was made to provide guidance for those people with an interest in studying the townland where their ancestor lived.

The book drew up a framework to assist its contributors in compiling their studies of eight townlands across Ulster: An overview of this framework is as follows:

1      Introduction
2      Location
3      History and tradition before the Plantation
4      Estates and the creation of farms
5      Population growth and decline
6      Housing Changes
7      Changing farming practices
8      Development of communications and markets
9      The community and its tradition

Brian Lambkin would like to see an agreed framework for the presentation of findings which will facilitate comparison of a series of townland studies. An objective of the *Connecting Our Place* Project will be to develop such a framework. It is intended to build a database capable of holding data of all types (political, economic, social) relating to the townlands of Ireland. This database would be capable of facilitating comparative study of all townlands.

To add interest to the family story I believe it is very worthwhile to find out as much as possible about the local history of an area associated with your ancestor. Ireland is well served by local history societies, many of which produce journals. In my own family history I knew that one ancestral home in Derrytrasna, near Lurgan, County Armagh was a linen receiving centre in the age of the cottage weaving industry in the early part of the 19th century. *Review* the journal of the Craigavon Historical Society carried articles on the linen industry of the Lurgan area. From these articles I could build up a picture of the domestic linen industry.

From a street directory I knew that in 1870 a great grandfather was the teacher of a Church Educational Society school in Newtowncunningham, County Donegal. This led to a desire to understand more about the 19th century education system. Another article in a local history magazine informed me that the Church of Ireland, feeling threatened by the new non-denominational National school system which was set up in 1831 with government funding, established an organisation of its own, the Church Educational Society to manage schools.

I think the persistence, dedication, enthusiasm and success of the local historian in Ireland can be demonstrated by the efforts of people such as Rev Mullin and his wife, Julia. If your ancestors originated in that part of County Londonderry between the towns of Limavady and Coleraine I can think of no better place to begin your family history research than an examination of their publications. Julia Mullin, for example, has researched and compiled two very detailed books on the histories of 46 Presbyterian Congregations located in the Presbyteries of Limavady and Coleraine. The value of her book *The Presbytery of Limavady* (North West Books, Limavady, 1989) is further enhanced by a detailed index of persons. In researching her book *The Presbytery of Coleraine* (published 1979) the range of record sources and record offices she accessed was quite formidable. The Presbyterian Historical Society, the Public Record Office of Northern Ireland and the Coleraine Chronicle (the local newspaper) provided most of her raw material. She examined, for example, the Route Presbytery Minutes from 1701-1706 and from 1811 -1834 and the Coleraine Presbytery Minutes from 1834 onwards.

As manager of the Derry Genealogy Centre my first step in any examination of a client's ancestry from the district of Aghadowey, County Londonderry was not our extensive database; it was a book, *Aghadowey A Parish and its Linen Industry* which was compiled and published by Rev T H Mullin in 1972.

In researching, for example, the Knox family of Aghadowey Rev Mullin's book recorded that John Knox, a linen merchant with a bleach green extending to 25 acres at Rushbrook in the townland of Ballynacally was one of the original investors in the Northern Banking Company when it was established in 1824. He bought 10 shares costing £1,000 (which was a considerable sum in those days).

The appendixes to Rev Mullin's book contained extracts from a number of sources. For example, Pyke's Survey of Aghadowey parish in 1725 recorded tenants by the names of John Knox and William Knox at Bwalla O'Hagan. In 1765, Alsop's Survey of the parish recorded a Robert Knox as a tenant at Clarehill.

In this case the persistence of the local historian has provided the family historian with much raw material. For example in examining the letters and accounts of the Agent of the Ironmongers' Company (the major landowner in the area) Rev Mullin discovered surveys of the estate dated 1725 and 1765. In the research room of the Registry of Deeds in Dublin he examined the lands index for any deeds relating to townlands where bleach greens existed in order to build up a picture of the prominent families involved in the linen trade in this parish. Many more sources were consulted and the end product is an indexed book containing many family histories.

In his introductory chapter, outlining the sources he consulted, the Rev Mullin states: "These, then, are some of the major sources on which is based this story of a rural community, a microcosm of the Ulster scene. My aim is to show the community as it is, its past enfolded in its present." The experienced researcher, who perhaps believes they are running out of options to explore in their family history quest, could gain much inspiration and hope from a book such as this.

In February 1999 Rev Mullin handed over much of his research work to the Irish Room at County Hall, Coleraine, County Londonderry. The "Rev T H Mullin

Collection" holds much material of value to the family historian including an analysis of names recorded in the Muster Rolls of 1622 and 1630, Rents Rolls of 1640, 1674 and 1738, Hearth Money Rolls of 1663 and Tithes of 1690/1691 for Coleraine.

I would recommend that in researching your ancestors you should attempt to identify any books that have been written about the area of interest to you. Not only will they provide much detailed information about the area and give insight into sources to search, but they may hold some information about your ancestor.

In conducting research, for example, in the Inishowen Peninsula, County Donegal, I continually refer to a number of books. *Three Hundred Years in Inishowen* by Amy Isabel Young which was published in 1929 records detailed family trees of the prominent families in this district. Harry Percival Swan produced two glorious books, in content and illustrations, on Inishowen: *Romantic Inishowen* (published Dublin, 1948) and *Twixt Foyle and Swilly* (Dublin, 1949).

In 1867 Michael Harkin, school teacher and postmaster, of Tirnaleague, Carndonagh under his pen name "Maghtochair" published *Inishowen Its History, Traditions and Antiquities.* Reprinted in 1985, publisher Peggy Harkin Simpson records that her grandfather "gathered a lot of information from the leading seanachies of Inishowen. He travelled around on a jaunting car and was a familiar figure in the remote parts of the peninsula."

On winters' evenings during the late 1940s and early 1950s Patrick Kavanagh, a teacher, of Clonmany recorded the stories told to him by his neighbour and friend Charles McGlinchey, weaver and tailor, who lived from 1861 to 1954. These memoirs were recorded in the book *The Last of the Name* (published by Blackstaff Press, Belfast, 1986). In Brian Friel's words Charles McGlinchey "by his concentration on the everyday, the domestic, the familiar, ... the momentous daily trivia of the world of his parish, he does give us an exact and lucid picture of profound transition". The book contains chapters on matters such as Poteen, Emigration, The Parish, Landlords and Tenants, and Faction Fights.

In 1998 Inishowen Rural Development Ltd part-sponsored a book by my father Sam Mitchell, *COUNTRY ROADS Walks on Foyleside and Inishowen.* "This is a 'Walks' book with a difference. Instead of mountain tracks and rocky trails, most of the walks are quiet country road circuits of 3 to 5 miles in length." This book tells you about the landscape and history of the area as you meet it on your walk. In all 20 walks are described and mapped for different parts of Inishowen.

The study of local history has also been accompanied by increased status in the academic world. Oxford University, for example, now offers a Diploma in Local History via the Internet (details at www.conted.ox.ac.uk/courses/lhist1). This one-year programme consists of two modules, one dealing with concepts and methods for local history and, the other with databases for historians. The main requirements for entrants are stated as "enthusiasm, commitment and some experience". In other words the sources, methods and personal qualities of the local historian are virtually identical to those of the family historian.

Donald Harman Akenson in his introduction to Bruce Elliott's book *Irish Migration in the Canadas A New Approach* (McGill-Queen's University Press, Kingston and Montreal, 1988) believed that Bruce Elliott's study which traced the movements of 775 Protestant families from North Tipperary to the London and Ottawa districts of Upper Canada (ie Ontario) in the period 1815-1855 was a breakthrough. Elliott traced "with precision the life paths of hundreds of individual migrants, pinpointing their place of origin in the Old World and tracing with equal precision their life course in the New. This is done with a significant number of individuals drawn from a similar background, so that one can generalize about the migration process as it occurred in this group." In short academics have much to gain from applying the techniques of local history and genealogical research.

There are a growing number of publishers catering for the local history market. Irish Academic Press, in association with St Patrick's College, Maynooth has begun to compile a series of pamphlets on various aspects of Irish local history (details on the Internet at www.iap.ie/lochist).

Geography Publications (details at www.may.ie/academic/geography/publications), since 1985, have been publishing their prestigious County History and Society Series. In the Preface to *Derry and Londonderry History and Society* (published in 1999) Seamus Heaney wrote "This book is the twelfth in the Irish County History series, one of the most important and sustained publishing enterprises ever carried through in this country. The volumes are marked by a unique combination of local interest and scholarly rigour...They will always be cherished, as a treasure trove of existing knowledge and new research, and they will never be out of date...This book widens and deepens and keeps opening knowledge into further knowledge, heritage into heritage, language into language, land into lore into learning." Other titles in the series, to date, are Cork, Donegal, Down, Dublin, Galway, Kilkenny, Offaly, Tipperary, Waterford, Wexford and Wicklow.

The Ulster Historical Foundation also publish an extensive collection of titles under the headings Historical Series, Local and Family History series, Educational Series and Gravestone Inscription Series. The aim of the Local and Family History Series is to provide a mechanism through which local historians, genealogists, societies and community groups can have their research published professionally and distributed both in Ireland and abroad. The Foundation maintains a website at www.ancestryireland.com.

Bookshops in Ireland stock a comprehensive range of local history books. Bookshops such as Kennys of Galway provide an online service (details at www.kennys.ie).

There is a strong network of local history societies in Ireland. For example the Federation for Ulster Local Studies (details at http://users.d-n-a.net/UlsterHistory/federation) which links historical societies in the nine counties of Ulster was set up to promote the study and recording of the history, antiquities and folk-life of Ulster. In researching your family history it makes sense to identify if a local history society exists in the area associated with your ancestor. Many of these societies produce journals and publications. For example I suspected that one of my ancestors died in the Draperstown area of County Londonderry. It was a member of the Ballinascreen Historical Society (based in Draperstown) who informed me that there existed a relevant headstone in the graveyard of Draperstown Church of Ireland Church. I might never have found this headstone without their help, as the headstone was badly weathered and difficult to read.

It goes without saying that local libraries in Ireland and the national institutions, such as the National Archives in Dublin and the Public Record Office of Northern Ireland in Belfast, hold a vast collection of records of relevance to the local historian and family historian. PRONI's website (http://proni.nics.gov.uk), for example, contains an online Geographical Index which will help you locate your County, Parish or Townland and provide an Ordnance Survey Map reference number. PRONI have also produced a series of information sheets under the headings of Local History; Your Family Tree; and Home-coming Series.

There are many more examples of organisations becoming involved in local history. The BBC, as part of its History 2000 initiative, is working with partners in the local community to build up an interactive website dedicated to bringing history to life. The Website can be accessed at www.bbc.co.uk/history.

Donegal County Council in association with others have established a project called **DL-NET** to collect, record and make accessible arts and heritage material of local interest via online public access computers and in due course through the Internet.

In short local history is a big growth area in Ireland and, I would see building up a picture of the local history of an area as an integral part of any search for ancestors.

# INDEX

www.ingramcontent.com/pod-product-compliance
Lightning Source LLC
Chambersburg PA
CBHW080338270326
41927CB00014B/3280